Essential Weight Loss Air Fryer Cookbook

Teaches 1000 New, Delicious, Quick & Easy, Low Carb Air Fryer Recipes for Effective Weight Loss, Keto & Healthy Living with Nutritional Facts for Beginners

Sussy Fisch

DEDICATION

This cookbook is dedicated to God Almighty for inspiring me to write this book. I also dedicate this cookbook to all who are on low carb weight loss and keto diet plan who use air fryer.

Table of Contents

INTRODUCTION

Air fryer is the healthiest gadget for preparing not only low fat meals, but also low carb recipes for those on weight loss and ketogenic lifestyles. If you want a live a healthy lifestyle or maintain your body size after shedding off excess weight, these 1000 low carb air fryer recipes revealed in this weight loss cookbook is all you need. These are the recipes and guides that helped me meet my weight loss target. Am sure it will also help you meet yours.

Here are the categories of recipes in this cookbook:

- **Air Fryer Beginner Tips**
- **Weight Loss and Low Carb Tips**
- **Keto Tips for Beginners**
- **Low Carb, Weight Loss Air Fryer Recipes** - For those on weight loss diet plan, who have not reached their weight loss target yet: **Appetizers, Breakfast, Main Dish, Side Dish, Dinner and Snack Air Fryer Recipes.**
- **Low Carb Keto Air Fryer Recipes** – Strictly for those living a ketogenic lifestyle who wish to reach their keto targets faster: **Breakfast, Beef, Poultry, Seafood, Veggies, Sides, Pork and Lamb Air Fryer Recipes.**
- **Healthy Low Carb Air Fryer Recipes** – For those who have reached their weight loss target and wish to maintain their new body structure. Also for diabetic patients and those who wish to adopt a healthy feeding lifestyle: **Breakfast, Main Dish, Side Dish, Healthy Air Fryer Recipes for Body Size Maintenance.**

Explore this cookbook and meet your weight loss target faster!

Love from,

Sussy Fisch

AIR FRYER BEGINNER TIPS

The problem with conventionally fried meals is that they contain excess fat. And eating fat is neither good for your live nor for your health. So being able to eat fries without the fat side is just a genius idea. For most fryers we must add a spoon of oil but it's really nothing compared to a conventional fryer and its liters of oil.

The oil-free fryer allows you to eat healthy fries that will not hinder your weight loss target.

Advantages of Air Fryers

A Multifunction Device

The other advantage of the air fryer is undoubtedly its versatility. So we can, of course, make fries and a lot more. Enjoy fat-free cooking and eat healthily! You can cook the following with most models:

- Poultry Dishes like Chicken legs, Turkey cutlets, etc.
- Vegetables
- Various desserts
- All kinds of nuggets
- Seafood
- Various donuts
- Simmered dishes

You will be able to cook almost anything

This is because most air fryers come with user manuals and cookbooks.

A Safe Fryer

The fryer full of boiling oil is a real danger especially if you have children. With the Oil-Free fryer, there is no risk of splashing or spilling!

Simple to Use

Contrary to what one might think, it is a very simple fryer to use. You put your chips in the tank, you pour a spoon of oil, you close the fryer, you select your program, the total time required to cook, and you will enjoy with your guests or your family because the fryer deals alone with your fries.

Has Features to Make Your Life Easier

Depending on the model you buy, the Oil-Free fryer is often designed to make your life easier. The programmer is convenient, as is the timer. The air fryer will soon become your kitchen clerk!

Easy Cleaning

Cleaning a conventional fryer is a chore and the work is stressful. Forget this nightmare with the air fryer. All removable items such as basket or bowl are dishwasher safe!

A Capacity Adapted to Every Need

Do you live alone, as a couple, with children, or often entertain guests? Choose the capacity of your Oil-Free fryer for your future uses and needs. As an indication, a fryer with a capacity of 1 kilo allows you to make fries for 4 people.

Prices Fit Your Budget

Today, fryers have become affordable. So, of course, as for all devices, there are cheap as well as high-end, but if your budget is tight, there is inevitably a cheap fryer waiting for you.

Air Fryer Working Principle

The working principle of air fryer is very unique. While other kitchen appliances out there mostly rely on conduction for preparing meals, air fryers differentiate themselves by incorporating airflow into their cooking process in a technique called "convection." Using "rapid air technology," the air fryer can prepare meals quickly with a very minimal amount of oil.

The Rapid Air Technology

For those of you who are wondering what "rapid air technology" is, let me give you a brief overview. Once the air fryer has pulled in the air from outside, the appliance immediately superheats the air to a temperature of 392 degrees Fahrenheit, after which it is passed into a very specialized heating chamber where the actual cooking happens. This whole process is referred to as "rapid air technology" as it eliminates the need to use a heavy amount of oil during frying, baking, grilling or even roasting and completes the cooking over a very short period of time.

Structure of an Air Fryer

Different brands of air fryers out there will definitely have some "flair" of their own! However, the following features are common staples of every air fryer. In general, an air fryer consists of:

1. **The Cooking Chamber:** This is the actual chamber where the cooking takes place. The difference between various models usually comes in the form of holding capacity. Some air fryers have the capacity to hold two cooking baskets, while some can hold only one.
2. **Heating Element:** The heating element of an air fryer is the coil inside the fryer that produces the heat once electricity passes through it. Once the heating element reaches the desired temperature, air is passed through this coil, where it gets heated up and is passed towards the fan and grill.
3. **Fan and Grill:** The fan and grill of the air fryer work together in order to ensure that the heated air is distributed evenly throughout the cooking basket. The air fryer is able to adjust the direction of the air, which plays a significant role in cooking the meal consistently.
4. **Exhaust System:** The exhaust system of an air fryer is responsible for maintaining a stable internal pressure and preventing the buildup of any harmful air. Some air fryer models tend to have a filter installed with the exhaust that cleans the exhausted air, making it free from any harmful particles or unpleasant odors.
5. **Transferable Food Tray:** The food tray is also known as the cooking basket. This is where you place the food in the air fryer to be cooked. Some newer models of air fryers tend to include a cooking basket with multiple walls built inside. This makes the cooking baskets much more versatile and allows the users to

cook multiple items in one go. Some models even include a universal handle that allows the cooking basket to be handled with ease.

Basic Features of an Air Fryer

Again, different brands of air fryers tend to add something special regarding their functionality in order to make their device stand out. However, the following features are common to almost all air fryers.

- **Automated Temperature Control System:** This is one of the more crucial and essential elements of an air fryer. The automated temperature control system plays a great role in determining how the final product turns out. The automatic temperature control system allows the appliance to keep track of the temperature and turn off the system when the airflow reaches a specific temperature. This allows each and every meal to be created according to the user's personal preferences.
- **Digital Screen and Touch Panel:** In our modern "digitized" generation, touch screen and digital controls are generating all the buzz! If you don't have a device with a touch screen panel, then you might as well be living in the past! Air fryer manufacturers are fully aware of this trend and have recently added a fully functional touchscreen interface into many fryers! This allows the users to seamlessly control the device without any hassle.
- **A Convenient Buzzer:** Most air fryers come with a buzzer that makes it extremely simple for users to know whenever their meals are ready. When cooking with an air fryer, you won't have to stand in front of the device all day just to make sure that your meals aren't burnt! All you have to do is set the timer and your air fryer will let you know once the cooking is done!
- **An Assorted Selection of Cooking Presets:** Air fryer companies fully understand that the majority of their users are not amazing chefs or prodigies when it comes to cooking. Some people out there are still amateur, but they want to cook and prepare amazing meals. For these people, the air fryer comes with a plethora of different preset parameters that ensure it is easy for inexperienced individuals to cook meals they can be proud of.

Preset Button Cooking Buttons with Temperature and Time

- **French fries** 400 degrees F 20 minutes
- **Roasts** 370 degrees F 15 minutes
- **Shrimp** 330 degrees F 15 minutes
- **Baked Goods** 350 degrees F 25 minutes
- **Chicken** 380 degrees F 25 minutes
- **Steak** 380 degrees F 25 minutes
- **Fish** 390 degrees F 25 minutes

Benefits of Using an Air Fryer

1. Preparing meals using an air fryer will reduce the amount of oil used by 80%, but that's not the only advantage here. An air fryer is very convenient and easy to use.
2. Cleaning an air fryer does not make any mess.

3. Oil- free meals produced by the air fryer will help with weight loss and improve overall health.
4. Cooking with an air fryer will allow you to cook meals rapidly.
5. Cleaning Instructions and Some Helpful Tips
6. Some people think that cleaning an air fryer might be an exceptionally herculean task! However, cleaning an air fryer is actually very easy.

Just make sure to keep the following steps in mind after use:

1. Remove the plug from the wall and give your air fryer time to cool down.
2. Gently wipe the external parts of the air fryer using a moist cloth (dipped in a mixture of water and mild detergent).
3. Clean the outer basket of the air fryer using hot water mixed with mild detergent and a soft sponge.
7. If you see that any residual food particles are stuck to the heating element, use a dish cleaning brush to remove them.

Some Additional Tips to Note When Cleaning the Appliance:

- For maximum efficiency, soak the basket with water and dish detergent for a few minutes and rinse it thoroughly under hot water.
- Keep in mind that metal utensils and cleaning brushes may leave scratches on the body of the fryer, so refrain from using brushes, sponges or harsh products on the air fryer and its parts.

Common Mistakes to Avoid when Using Air Fryers

- If you are just getting comfortable with your new air fryer, then you should really follow the following tips to increase the longevity of your device:
- Make sure to keep your device in a well-ventilated place for maximum airflow. Keeping your air fryer in a corner will restrict airflow, which will damage your device in the long run.
- When you are not using your air fryer, make sure to remove the power cables to prevent any internal damage.
- Keep in mind that the air fryer does not take long to heat up, so preheat it just before cooking.
- When using frozen foods, make sure to thaw them thoroughly before placing them in your cooking basket (unless specifically asked by a recipe).

Air Frying Basic Steps

1. Take your cooking basket and drizzle a bit of oil in it.
2. Prepare the ingredients of the meal accordingly.
3. Transfer the prepared tray to your cooking basket and follow any additional instructions.
4. Alternatively, if you are baking a cake then you might want to put the batter in a separate dish and place this inside your cooking tray.
5. Set your temperature to the specified temperature and set your timer.
6. Make sure to check if the recipe requires you to shake your basket. If so, do it accordingly.
7. Wait until the timer runs out. Enjoy!

Note that most recipes will require little to no oil! Overall, the oil intake will be lowered by almost 80%.

Some Healthy Recommended Oils

If you want to maximize the "health" factor of your meals, it is of paramount importance that you use the healthiest oil possible! To save you some time and effort, I have listed the five healthiest oil that you can use while cooking using your air fryer.

1. **Coconut Oil:** When it comes to high heat cooking, coconut oil is the best with over 90% of the fatty acids being saturated, which makes it very resistant to heat. This particular oil is semi-solid at room temperature and can be used for months without it turning rancid. This particular oil also has a lot of health benefits! Since this oil is rich in a fatty acid known as lauric acid, it can help to improve cholesterol levels and kill various pathogens.
2. **Extra-Virgin Olive Oil:** Olive oil is very well known for its heart health benefits. In fact, this is one of the main reasons why the Mediterranean diet uses olive oil as a key ingredient. Some recent studies have shown that olive oil can even help to improve health biomarkers such as increasing HDL cholesterol and lowering the amount of bad LDL cholesterol.
3. **Avocado Oil:** The composition of Avocado oil is very similar to olive oil and as such it holds similar health benefits. It can be used for many purposes including as an alternative to olive oil.
4. **Fish Oil:** Fish oil is extremely rich in omega-3 fatty acids such as EPA and DHA. Just a tablespoon of fish oil is enough to satisfy the body's daily needs. If you are looking for the best fish oil, then cod fish liver oil is your best option—plus, it I also rich in Vitamin D3. But here is the thing, since fish oil has a high concentration of polyunsaturated fats, it should not be used for cooking. The best way to use this oil is as a supplement.
5. **Grape seed Oil:** Grape seed oil is a very versatile cooking oil that is extracted from grape seeds that are left behind after winemaking. This is a favorite oil among chefs and foodies!
   This oil has a very mild flavor that can be added with other ingredients that give a very strong flavor to meals. Grape seed has a very high percentage of polyunsaturated fat and has a similar fatty acid profile to soybean oil. According to multiple sources, grape seed oil has a good number of positive effects on the heart.

COOKING TERMINOLOGIES

These are some of the cooking terms I will be using from time to time. It is good to familiarize yourself with these terminologies now. I also included some measurements. I may not have used all these terms in this book because I listed them before I started writing the manuscript.

1. **Beat:** To use a spoon, a fork, a whisk, or an electric mixer to mix ingredients together, using a fast circular movement
2. **Blend:** To combine two or more ingredients until the mixture is smooth and uniform in texture, color, and flavor
3. **Bread:** To coat a food in bread crumbs before frying or baking
4. **Chill:** To put the food in the refrigerator for at least 2 hours
5. **Chop:** To cut into little pieces
6. **Combine:** To put items together or place them in the same bowl
7. **Dice:** To cut into small square pieces
8. **Drain:** To remove all the liquid—may be done in a colander, strainer or by pressing a plate against the food while tilting the container forward
9. **Fold:** To gently combine a light, delicate substance (such as beaten egg whites) with a heavier mixture, using a light "over-and–under" motion
10. **Grate:** To scrape against the small holes of a grater, making thin little pieces
11. **Grease:** To coat a pan with oil or margarine so food does not stick when cooking
12. **Marinate:** To soak foods in a flavorful liquid that tenderizes or adds flavor to meat, fish, chicken, veggies, or tofu
13. **Mash:** To squash food with a fork, spoon, or masher
14. **Melt:** To use heat to make a solid into a liquid
15. **Mince:** To cut into very small pieces, smaller than chopped or diced
16. **Mix:** To stir together with a spoon, fork, or electric mixer
17. **Peel:** To remove the outside of a fruit or vegetable
18. **Pit:** To remove the seed
19. **Preheat:** To turn your oven on ahead of time so it heats up to the temperature you need it to be before cooking
20. **Shred:** To scrape against the large holes on a grater, making long, thin pieces
21. **Stir:** To mix with a spoon
22. **Strain:** To remove solid bits from liquid
23. **Wash:** To clean thoroughly (Fresh fruits that do not have skins to peel and all fresh veggies need to be cleaned with a special brush before using.)
24. **Whisk:** To use a whisk to quickly stir to get lumps out
25. **Bake:** To cook in an oven
26. **Boil:** To heat on the stove until the liquid gets hot enough for bubbles to rise and break the surface
27. **Broil:** To cook by direct heat in the broiler of an electric or gas range
28. **Brown:** To cook until the color of the food changes to brown
29. **Fry:** To cook food in hot fat such as olive oil or butter ("deep fry" means to put enough fat in the pan to cover the food)
30. **Roast:** The same as bake, but this term is used with cooking meat
31. **Sauté:** To cook quickly in a little oil, butter, or margarine
32. **Scramble:** To mix up really well (to scramble eggs, stir while they cook)

33. **Simmer:** To cook in liquid over low heat just below the boiling point (bubbles form slowly and burst before reaching the surface)
34. **Steam:** To cook food using the heat from boiling water without putting the food directly in the water—usually done with a device called a steamer (a silver bowl with holes that folds to fit many different pans)
35. **Stew:** To cook food for a long time in a covered pan, with liquid.
36. **Stir-fry:** To toss and stir cut-up pieces of food in a pan with hot oil, cooking it quickly.

VOLUME EQUIVALENT AND WEIGHT CONVERSION

Abbreviations

- Table spoon---tbsp.
- Tea spoon---tsp.
- Pound---lb.
- Ounce---oz.
- Gallon--gal.

Conversions

- ¼ teaspoon = 1 ml
- ½ teaspoon = 2 ml
- 1 teaspoon = 5 ml
- 1 tablespoon = 15 ml
- ¼ cup = 59 ml
- ½ cup = 118 ml
- ½ ounce = 15 g
- 1 cup = 235 ml
- 1 ounce = 30 g
- 2 ounces = 60 g
- 4 ounces = 115 g
- 8 ounces = 225 g
- 12 ounces = 340 g
- 16 ounces or 1 lb. = 455 g

WEIGHT LOSS AND LOW CARB TIPS

About Low Carb Diet

Low Carb diets are those diets that provides the body with adequate carbohydrate for energy but not for storage.

When you eat food that's rich in carbohydrates, the body produces glucose and insulin. Glucose is converted by the body into usable energy. It is the body's most preferred energy source. Insulin is manufactured by the body to process the glucose.

When the body uses glucose for energy, it stores the fats inside the body. This is what causes weight gain. Excessive weight gain, as you know, can lead to a number of ailments, such as hypertension, heart disease, diabetes and so on.

By taking on a low-carb diet, the body is forced to undergo a state called **KETOSIS** - which is a process wherein the body produces ketones, which are the byproducts of fat breakdown in the liver. The ketones then become the primary source of energy, instead of carbohydrates. By using ketones as an energy source, the body benefits in more ways than one. This results not only in weight loss but also in better physical and mental performance. This is primarily how the low-carb diet works.

Advantages of Low Carb Diet Lifestyle

- Helps to treat Epilepsy
- Controls high blood pressure, cholesterol and heart diseases
- Helps you meet your weight loss goal
- Controls your blood sugar level and diabetes
- Improves your mental focus

It is a well-known fact that carbohydrates are important since they are the fuel that our body needs to function optimally; however, we need to be careful about the kind of carbohydrates we take or else you will find yourself always gaining weight even when you don't eat as much. So, how do you determine the kinds of carbohydrates to eat? Simple carbohydrates are easily and quickly digested, they have what is known as a high glycemic index.

This is a ranking on how fast a carbohydrate is converted into sugar in your body to produce energy for the body cells. Foods with high glycemic index can raise your blood sugar to very high levels than your body can manage. This can cause hormonal imbalance leading to the increased secretion of insulin, which helps regulate blood sugar level. Since insulin is also a fat storing hormone, high amounts of insulin in the body will necessitate the storage of more fat for energy. This will lead to rapid weight gain and obesity, and also creates the need for everyone to check on their carbohydrate intake to avoid the health risks that may accompany a high carbohydrate diet.

Foods with high carbohydrate content are referred to as fast-carbs and should be avoided, as they can be a ticking time bomb. If you adopt a regular habit of consuming fast carbs, you will develop a high risk of developing type 2 diabetes, excessive and rapid weight gain or obesity, which might lead to a lot more other health risks such as high blood pressure and cardiovascular diseases.

Most processed foods fall under this category of simple carbs or fast carbs and should be given at all costs. It is advisable to develop a low carb diet lifestyle by only consuming healthy foods with a low glycemic index, as not all foods with low glycemic index are healthy. For instance, while baked potatoes have a higher glycemic index as opposed to potato chips, baked potatoes are a far much healthier option. If you have to take carbohydrates, then embrace complex carbohydrates high in fiber and which take a long time to be digested hence not causing spikes in the blood sugar levels. While adopting a low carb diet is exiting, most people don't have time to cook and they easily go back to their poor eating habit.

Therefore, slow cookers are the secret weapon behind the perfect working of the low carb recipes. They make it possible to cook foods for long durations at low temperatures while maintaining their rich taste and compromise less on the quality of nutrients in the cooked foods unlike with the case of fast cooking.

Foods That Should Be limited From Your Meal

- **Grains** are quite fattening especially Gluten grains like barley and wheat. Oaths and Rice are healthier alternatives.
- **Processed foods** generally are no advisable to consume. They have low nutrients value and might contain some harmful additives. Trans fat containing foods are unhealthy and found in many processed foods.
- **Alcohols** like Beer causes heavy weight gain if consumed excessively and are generally harmful to the health. However, a glass of wine or two is not harmful.
- **Sugar** is the major cause of many disease like Diabetes and other heart ailments. Artificial calories are also no advisable even though they don't have calories.
- **Ice cream and Chocolates** should be consumed in a controlled amount and not frequent.
- **Deep-fried foods** like chips and French fries are also not good for your body as they contain a lot of calories
- **Sodas and minerals** should be limited too because they contain a lot of sugars and chemical as well

You must not necessarily cut off these foods from your diet but you should be much conscious on how much you consume them without feeling guilty about it later.

LOW CARB, WEIGHT LOSS AIR FRYER RECIPES

For those on weight loss diet plan, who have not reached their weight loss target yet.

Appetizer Recipes

Chicken Skewers in Yogurt

Servings: 2

Total Time: 40 Minutes

Calories: 130

Fat: 3 g

Protein: 20 g

Carbs: 5 g

Fiber: 1.3 g

Ingredients and Quantity

- 500 g chicken breast
- 1 tsp. turmeric
- A pinch strong pepper
- 1/2 tsp. cumin powder
- 1/2 tsp. coriander powder
- Some small onions
- 2 tsp. yogurt with 0% fat
- 1/2 lemon
- Black pepper and salt, to taste

Direction

1. Cut the chicken breast into pieces.
2. Put them in a deep dish with the spices and yogurt. Mix well.
3. Cover and marinate for three hours in the refrigerator.
4. Drain the chicken pieces and put them on skewers, alternating with the onions previously cut in four.
5. Add black pepper along with salt.
6. Cook for 10 minutes on the air fryer grill.
7. During this time, peel and chop two onions and Sauté for 2 to 3 minutes in an air fryer at medium temperature.
8. Pass in a mixer along with the marinated total time required to prepare.
9. Heat gradually, without boiling.

10. Add black pepper along with salt and finish with some lemon juice.
11. Serve the skewers immediately with the accompanying sauce. Enjoy!

Green Vegetables with Cilantro and Parsley

Servings: 4

Total Time: 35 Minutes

Calories: 65

Fat: 1 g

Protein: 2 g

Carbs: 8 g

Fiber: 0.6 g

Ingredients and Quantity

- 2 slices eggplant
- 200 g fresh green beans
- 1/2 leek
- 1 sliced zucchini
- 1 sliced squash
- 1 celery stalk
- 1 julienne onion
- 1 parsley
- 1 packet chopped cilantro
- 1 vegetable broth sachet diluted with 200 ml warm water
- Salt, to taste

Direction

1. In an air fryer, sauté all vegetables in 200ml of vegetable broth for 15 minutes, stirring and observing them so that they are crispy.
2. Once the vegetables are cooked, add the chopped parsley and cilantro. Serve and enjoy!

Green Cabbage with Mint

Servings: 2

Total Time: 40 Minutes

Calories: 24

Fat: 0 g

Protein: 1 g

Carbs: 4 g

Fiber: 0.2 g

Ingredients and Quantity

- 1/2 green cabbage
- 1 package fresh mint
- 1 minced garlic clove
- 1 lemon
- 1 pinch salt

Direction

1. Wash and cut the cabbage and mint roughly.
2. Sauté garlic and salt in a pan with 500ml of water and cook in an air fryer for 20 minutes. Serve and enjoy!

Seasoned Chicken Skewers

Servings: 5

Total Time: 40 Minutes

Calories: 100

Fat: 4 g

Protein: 26 g

Carbs: 1 g

Fiber: 1 g

Ingredients and Quantity

- 1 kg chicken breast
- 250 ml 0% fat yogurt
- 1 tsp. ground pepper powder
- 1 tsp. turmeric
- 1 tsp. cumin powder
- 1 tsp. coriander powder
- 1 tsp. grated ginger
- 1 garlic clove, mashed

Direction

1. Dip 25 wooden skewers in a little water, so they don't burn while baking.
2. Remove fat from chicken breast and cut into pieces.
3. Prepare the sauce with the yogurt and the spices.
4. Put the chicken pieces on the skewers and, in a deep dish, make them completely soaked.
5. Leave several hours or a whole night in the fridge.
6. Then place the skewers on a grill or barbecue plate and cook in an air fryer for 8 to 10 minutes until the chicken is soft and golden. Serve and enjoy!

Thyme Chicken

Servings: 4

Total Time: 1 Hour 10 Minutes

Calories: 225

Fat: 10 g

Protein: 24 g

Carbs: 8 g

Fiber: 2.2 g

Ingredients and Quantity

- 1 whole chicken
- 1 pack fresh thyme
- 2 shallots
- 3 yogurts with 0% fat
- 1/2 lemon
- 1 packet parsley
- Some mint leaves
- 1 garlic clove
- Black pepper and salt, to taste

Direction

1. Cut chicken into pieces and season.
2. Add a good amount of water to the bottom compartment of a steaming pan, add salt and wait till it boils.
3. Spread half of thyme on top of pan.
4. Arrange the chicken pieces on the thyme.
5. Top with the rest of the thyme and the peeled and chopped shallots.
6. Close the lid and cook in an air fryer for 30 to 35 minutes from the moment steam starts to escape.
7. In the meantime, put the yogurts in a bowl, add the half lemon juice, the chopped and dried mint leaves, the finely cut garlic clove.
8. Add black pepper along with salt, set aside in the refrigerator until serving, as an accompaniment to the chicken. Enjoy!

Chicken with Yogurt

Servings: 4

Total Time: 1 Hour 45 Minutes

Calories: 285

Fat: 12 g

Protein: 26 g

Carbs: 5 g

Fiber: 2.8 g

Ingredients and Quantity

- 1 whole chicken
- 120 g chopped onion
- 2 fat-free yogurts
- 1/2 tsp. ginger powder
- 1/2 tsp. paprika
- 2 tsp. lemon juice
- 2 tsp. curry
- 1/2 lemon zest
- Black pepper and salt

Direction

1. Cut chicken, remove skin and place the pieces in a nonstick air fryer.
2. Put the remaining ingredients over the chicken and cover.
3. Let it cook in an air fryer for about 1 hour and 30 minutes over low heat.
4. Season to taste and, if necessary, remove the lid at the end of cooking to reduce the sauce.
5. Serve very hot. Enjoy!

Chicken with Ginger

Servings: 4

Total Time: 1 Hour 20 Minutes

Calories: 285

Fat: 12 g

Protein: 26 g

Carbs: 5 g

Fiber: 2.8 g

Ingredients and Quantity

- 1 whole chicken
- 2 large onions
- 3 garlic cloves
- Some cloves
- 5 g ginger
- Black pepper and salt, to taste

Direction

1. Cut chicken into pieces.

2. Sauté onions and garlic cloves, peeled and chopped in a lightly greased air fryer over low heat in the air fryer.
3. Add the chicken pieces to which the cloves will have been fixed. Cover with water.
4. Add the grated ginger, black pepper, along with salt.
5. Cook in an air fryer on medium heat until water evaporates. Serve and enjoy!

Sautéed Chicken with Pepper

Servings: 4

Total Time: 41 Minutes

Calories: 231

Fat: 5 g

Protein: 39 g

Carbs: 6 g

Fiber: 2.3 g

Ingredients and Quantity

- 4 chicken breasts
- 6 small red onions or shallots
- 3 to 6 fresh peppers
- 4 garlic cloves
- 1 piece fresh ginger
- 1 leaf lemon balm
- 150 ml water
- Black pepper and salt

Direction

1. Remove the skin from the chicken breasts and cut each into eight pieces vertically.
2. Chop the onion into thin strips for decoration of the dish. Wash and peel peppers, onions or shallots, garlic, ginger root, and lemon balm leaf.
3. Beat the peppers, half the ginger, and the lemon balm in a blender. Reserve.
4. Beat the onions, garlic, and other half of ginger until mashed.
5. In a lightly oiled nonstick frying pan, sauté the mashed pepper for 1 to 2 minutes.
6. Add the chicken pieces, mix so that they are well wrapped in the puree.
7. Add water and incorporate into onion puree. Season adequately using salt along with pepper.
8. Cook in an air fryer over high heat for 5 minutes with the air fryer uncapped.
9. Serve hot with onion slices for decoration. Enjoy!

Turnip Curry Soup

Servings: 2

Total Time: 1 Hour 5 Minutes

Calories: 193

Fat: 9 g

Protein: 6 g

Carbs: 8 g

Fiber: 1.9 g

Ingredients and Quantity

- 1 kg turnip
- 1 onion
- 4 garlic cloves
- 1 pinch curry powder
- 900 ml lean chicken broth
- A few drops tabasco
- 1/2 lemon
- 200 g fat free yogurt
- 70 g thin slices nonfat ham
- 2 sprigs finely chopped parsley or chives
- 1 pinch nutmeg
- Black pepper and salt

Direction

1. Peel and remove the central and hardest part of the turnips.
2. Peel the onion and chop it roughly.
3. Peel the cloves of garlic and chop.
4. Sauté onion and garlic at medium temperature.
5. Cover and cook for 5 minutes, and then add the turnips.
6. Mix, cover, and cook for 10 minutes in the air fryer.
7. Add the curry, mix well, and add the broth.
8. Cook for about 30 minutes until it begins to boil.
9. Beat everything in a blender: the soup should be very thin. Heat the spice.
10. Add a few drops of tabasco and half lemon juice.
11. Heat in the air fryer and add 150g of yogurt.
12. Meanwhile, fry the ham in its own broth in a frying pan.
13. Drain, transfer it to a sheet of paper towels, and crumple it with your fingers.
14. Serve the soup with some yogurt, sprinkle bacon, parsley, and nutmeg. Enjoy!

Eggplant Salad

Servings: 2

Total Time: 35 Minutes

Calories: 133

Fat: 12 g

Protein: 3 g

Carbs: 5 g

Fiber: 1.3 g

Ingredients and Quantity

- 2 large eggplants
- 1 tsp. vinegar
- 1 garlic clove
- 4 spring onions
- 1 shallot
- 2 parsley stalks
- Black pepper and salt

Direction

1. Peel and cut the eggplants into large pieces.
2. Cook in the air fryer over high heat with boiling water for about 20 minutes.
3. Lower the heat and cook for another 20 minutes.
4. Let cool and crush with a fork.
5. Drizzle the eggplant with a well-seasoned vinaigrette dressing with chopped garlic, chives, and shallot in very small pieces.
6. Sprinkle the chopped parsley and serve very cold. Enjoy!

Greek-Style Lemon Soup

Servings: 2

Total Time: 20 Minutes

Calories: 70

Fat: 0 g

Protein: 6 g

Carbs: 10 g

Fiber: 0.7 g

Ingredients and Quantity

- 1 L water
- 2 cubes fat-free chicken broth
- 1 pinch saffron
- 2 carrots
- 2 zucchinis
- 2 egg yolks
- 1 lemon

Direction

1. Boil water with the chicken broth cubes and saffron.
2. Meanwhile, grate the carrot and zucchini roughly.
3. Add the carrot to the broth and simmer for 5 minutes.
4. Add zucchini and boil for 3 minutes.
5. Add one or two egg yolks, zest, and lemon juice.
6. Keep on medium heat in the air fryer so as not to boil anymore. Serve and enjoy!

Zucchini Tajine

Servings: 2

Total Time: 60 Minutes

Calories: 207

Fat: 16 g

Protein: 9 g

Carbs: 6 g

Fiber: 2 g

Ingredients and Quantity

- 2 garlic cloves
- 1 tsp. cumin powder
- 1 tsp. coriander powder
- 1 tsp. garam masala powder
- 500 ml water
- 1 cube chicken broth without fat
- 2 tbsp. tomato paste
- 4 zucchinis

For Garnishing:

- 1 lemon
- 1 bunch coriander

Direction

1. Sauté minced garlic and spices in a large saucepan in the air fryer over low heat for a few minutes.
2. Add the water, the chicken stock cube, the tomato extract, and the sliced zucchini.
3. Cook for 35 minutes at medium temperature topped with pan and serve it with lemon and cilantro sauce, if possible, in a tajine pan. Enjoy!

Eggplant Terrine

Servings: 4

Total Time: 1 Hour 50 Minutes

Calories: 262

Fat: 27 g

Protein: 15 g

Carbs: 6 g

Fiber: 2 g

Ingredients and Quantity

- 2 eggplants
- 100 g chicken or turkey ham
- 3 sprigs celery1 garlic clove
- 3 sprigs chopped parsley
- 3 tomatoes

Direction

1. Slice the eggplants and sprinkle salt to remove excess water.
2. Sauté diced ham in the air fryer.
3. Reserve. Save the cooking stock for the vegetables.
4. Cut the celery branches and sauté them in the pan over low heat.
5. Mix ham and celery.
6. In an air fryer proof dish, make a layer of sliced eggplant, one with a mixture of chopped ham, celery, parsley, and garlic, one with sliced tomatoes, and one with the remaining eggplant slices.
7. Cook for 1 hour at 180 degrees. Serve and enjoy!

Garden Terrine

Servings: 4

Total Time: 30 Minutes

Calories: 300

Fat: 21 g

Protein: 15 g

Carbs: 6 g

Fiber: 3 g

Ingredients and Quantity

- 900 g carrots
- 500 g leeks
- 5 beaten eggs
- 125 g 0% fat cottage chees
- 100 g chopped nonfat ham
- Black pepper and salt

Direction

1. Steam the leek beforehand.
2. Grate the carrot and beat previously cooked leek in a blender.
3. Mix in beaten eggs, cottage cheese, black pepper, along with salt.
4. Add the vegetables, mix well, and put them in a rectangular pan.
5. Cook in the air fryer without lid in the preheated air fryer to 190 degrees, and follow the cooking regularly. Serve and enjoy!

Parsley Tomatoes

Servings: 2

Total Time: 28 Minutes

Calories: 57

Fat: 0 g

Protein: 3 g

Carbs: 6 g

Fiber: 0.5 g

Ingredients and Quantity

- 4 ripe tomatoes
- 1 red or white onion, cut into 8 equal parts
- 2 minced garlic cloves
- 5 jalapeno peppers
- 1 1/2 L lemon juice
- Some coriander stalks
- A pinch salt

Direction

1. Cook tomatoes in the air fryer for 30 seconds.
2. Peel and remove the seeds in the mixer container.
3. Put the onion pieces, the garlic, and the salt.
4. Remove the peduncle from the jalapeno peppers and cut them in two.
5. Save some seeds for a more or less spicy sauce.
6. Cut the peppers roughly and add the desired amount of seeds to the mixer bowl.
7. Grind until the sauce reaches the desired consistency.
8. Transfer the sauce to a pan and cook in the air fryer at medium temperature until it is covered in a pink foam, which should take about 6 to 8 minutes to cook.
9. Remove from heat and let cool for at least 10 minutes.
10. Add lemon juice and coriander. Serve and enjoy!

Eggplants with Garlic and Parsley

Servings: 2

Total Time: 50 Minutes

Calories: 110

Fat: 10 g

Protein: 1 g

Carbs: 3 g

Fiber: 1.1 g

Ingredients and Quantity

- 200 to 250 g eggplant
- 1 garlic clove
- 2 parsley stalks
- Black pepper and salt, to taste

Direction

1. Remove the stalks, wash, and dry the eggplants.
2. Cut them in two lengthwise. Remove the pulp from the eggplants.
3. Chop the garlic, parsley and eggplant pulp.
4. Season adequately using salt along with pepper.
5. Fill the eggplants with the mixture.
6. Close them in foil and cook in the air fryer for about 30 to 35 minutes at 170 degrees. Serve and enjoy!

Air Fryer Eggplants

Servings: 1

Total Time: 45 Minutes

Calories: 110

Fat: 10 g

Protein: 1 g

Carbs: 3 g

Fiber: 1.1 g

Ingredients and Quantity

- 1 eggplant
- 1 tomato
- 1 medium onion
- 1 garlic clove
- 2 thyme stems

- 1 tbsp. basil
- Black pepper and salt, to taste

Direction

1. Wash and dice the eggplant. Wash and mash the tomato.
2. Peel the onion and chop the garlic.
3. Sauté onion with some water until translucent.
4. Add the eggplant and brown in the air fryer over high heat and then medium.
5. Add the tomatoes, garlic, thyme, and basil.
6. Season adequately using salt along with pepper.
7. Cover and cook in the air fryer for 30 minutes over low heat. Serve and enjoy!

Vegetable Broth

Servings: 1

Total Time: 21 Minutes

Calories: 70

Fat: 5 g

Protein: 2 g

Carbs: 4 g

Fiber: 0.7 g

Ingredients and Quantity

- 50 g carrots
- 50 g mushrooms
- 25 g celery sprigs
- 25 g leeks, white
- 2 medium tomatoes
- 1 1/4 L fat free chicken broth
- 1 packet parsley
- Salt and pepper, to taste

Direction

1. Cut the washed and peeled vegetables into very thin sticks. Cut the tomatoes in four.
2. Remove seeds and water, then roughly cut into cubes.
3. Wait till it boils in the air fryer, sprinkle black pepper and salt as per your taste.
4. Dip the vegetables (minus the tomatoes) in the stock and cook them in the air fryer without covering the pan for 5 to 6 minutes (the vegetables should be slightly crispy).
5. Remove the pan from the heat, add the tomato pieces and the finely chopped parsley.
6. Serve it hot. Enjoy!

Greek-Style Mushrooms

Servings: 2

Total Time: 32 Minutes

Calories: 60

Fat: 8 g

Protein: 5 g

Carbs: 2 g

Fiber: 0.7 g

Ingredients and Quantity

- 5 tsp. lemon juice
- 2 bay leaves
- 1 tsp. coriander seeds
- 1 tsp. black pepper
- 700 g mushrooms
- 4 tsp. minced parsley
- Salt, to taste

Direction

1. Add a liter of water in a saucepan with lemon juice, bay leaves, coriander seeds, and black pepper. Season with salt.
2. Wait till it boils and cook in the air fryer for 10 minutes.
3. Remove the grounded part of the champignon's feet. Wash quickly, drain and cut into pieces.
4. Add the mushrooms to the pan and wait for it to boil again.
5. Set 2 minutes and turn off the heat.
6. Add the parsley. Mix gently. Let it cool completely in the broth.
7. Drain the mushrooms, put them on a plate, and drizzle with the cooking broth, adding some coriander grains. Serve and enjoy!

Zucchini Fondue with Lobsters

Servings: 4

Total Time: 1 Hour 15 Minutes

Calories: 250

Fat: 17 g

Protein: 15 g

Carbs: 5 g

Fiber: 2.5 g

Ingredients and Quantity

- 1 kg cooked lobster
- 800 g zucchini
- 2 large onions
- 6 sprigs mint
- 1 tbsp. olive oil
- 1/2 lemon juice
- Salt and pepper, to taste
- Gray coarse sea salt, or common coarse salt

Direction

1. Wash the zucchini, dry, peel, and cut into 5mm strips.
2. Peel and chop the onions. Heat the olive oil in a pan and Sauté the onion.
3. Add the zucchini, salt along with pepper, mix and cook in the air fryer for 40 minutes, stir the total time required to prepare occasionally so as not to stick to the bottom, and when the mixture becomes tender, add the lemon juice and minced mint.
4. Arrange zucchini fondue and lobster meat on a serving platter. Enjoy!

Cooked Tuna

Servings: 4

Total Time: 25 Minutes

Calories: 128

Fat: 3 g

Protein: 24 g

Carbs: 0 g

Fiber: 1.2 g

Ingredients and Quantity

- 2 parsley leaves
- 1 small packet fresh oregano
- 1 small packet thyme
- 3 to 4 bay leaves
- 1 lemon
- 1 tsp. mustard seed
- 1 tuna slice, about 400 to 500 g

Direction

1. In a container, finely chop herbs and mash bay leaves.
2. Add lemon juice and mustard grains. Mix well.
3. Pass both sides of the tuna slice in the marinade.

4. Cook the fish in the air fryer for 5 minutes (or in a lightly oiled frying pan) on each side over high heat and drizzle with the marinade. Serve and enjoy!

Crab Crepes

Servings: 2

Total Time: 12 Minutes

Calories: 225

Fat: 10 g

Protein: 18 g

Carbs: 3 g

Fiber: 2.2 g

Ingredients and Quantity

- 3 eggs
- 170 g shredded crab meat
- 2 tbsp. mustard

Direction

1. Mix ingredients, make balls and crush with the palm of your hand to flatten into a disc.
2. Cook in an air fryer for 10 minutes. Serve and enjoy!

Small Crab Puddings

Servings: 5

Total Time: 55 Minutes

Calories: 115

Fat: 4 g

Protein: 21 g

Carbs: 1 g

Fiber: 1.1 g

Ingredients and Quantity

- 200 g sliced smoked salmon
- 2 eggs
- 1 tbsp. cornstarch
- 350 ml milk
- 200 g crab meat
- A little cube fish broth

- Black pepper and salt

Direction

1. Distribute the salmon slices Smoked in little bowls.
2. Beat eggs, cornstarch diluted in milk, and then crab meat. Season the fish stock with black pepper along with salt.
3. Cook in an air fryer for 45 minutes at 180 degrees. Serve and enjoy!

Chicken Kebabs with Mustard

Servings: 4

Total Time: 35 Minutes

Calories: 250

Fat: 20 g

Protein: 15 g

Carbs: 0 g

Fiber: 2.5 g

Ingredients and Quantity

- 4 chicken breasts
- 2 tbsp. strong mustard
- 1 tsp. lemon juice
- 1/2 garlic cloves, crushed
- 250 ml hot water
- 1 cube nonfat chicken broth
- 500 ml skimmed milk
- 1 tbsp. cornstarch

Direction

1. Cut the chicken breasts into large pieces and place them in a container.
2. In a bowl, combine mustard, lemon juice, garlic, and hot water mixture with chicken stock.
3. Drizzle the chicken with three-quarters of the sauce.
4. Mix well and refrigerate for 2 hours.
5. After 2 hours, put the chicken pieces on skewers and cook at 200 degrees to cook for 15 minutes.
6. In a small saucepan, add the remaining sauce and milk (in which cornstarch should be mixed).
7. Bring the pan to a low heat to thicken the sauce. Serve and enjoy!

Breakfast Recipes

Scrambled Eggs with Crab

Servings: 4

Total Time: 20 Minutes

Calories: 313

Fat: 21 g

Protein: 28 g

Carbs: 2 g

Fiber: 0.9 g

Ingredients and Quantity

- 6 medium eggs
- 2 tbsp. fish sauce
- 100 g crab meat
- 2 medium shallots

Direction

1. In a bowl, lightly beat eggs and fish sauce.
2. Drain the water from the crab meat well.
3. Peel the shallots.
4. Sauté the shallots for one minute in the air fryer until golden. Then add the eggs.
5. Sauté the crab until it is slightly golden. Then add the eggs and mix.
6. Cook the mixture for 3 to 5 minutes at medium temperature until golden brown.
7. Take out from the air fryer and serve hot. Enjoy!

Eggs in Mini Casseroles with Salmon

Servings: 6

Total Time: 15 Minutes

Calories: 250

Fat: 30 g

Protein: 16 g

Carbs: 2 g

Fiber: 0.7 g

Ingredients and Quantity

- 12 tsp. 0% fat cottage cheese

- Chopped tarragon
- 2 large slices of smoked salmon
- 6 eggs
- Black pepper and salt, to taste
- 6 medium size bowl

Direction

1. In each bowl, add 2 teaspoons cottage cheese and a hint of tarragon.
2. Cut each slice of salmon into three and add in each bowl. Then add an egg.
3. Arrange the bowls in the air fryer.
4. Cover and cook for 3 to 5 minutes at medium temperature.

Note: Salmon can be substituted for ham, turkey breast, or any other protein of your liking.

Salted Pancakes

Servings: 1

Total Time: 55 Minutes

Calories: 55

Fat: 2 g

Protein: 6 g

Carbs: 5 g

Fiber: 1 g

Ingredients and Quantity

For the Pancake Base:

- 2 tbsp. oat bran
- 1 tbsp. wheat bran
- 1 tbsp. 0% fat cream cheese
- 3 eggs, with egg whites beaten in peaks
- Black pepper and salt

Optional Ingredients:

- 185 g crushed tuna
- 200 g smoked salmon
- 150 g non-fat ham
- 150 g ground beef

Direction

1. Mix all pancake base ingredients (except the egg whites) until smooth.
2. Add salt and black pepper to taste.
3. Then add the ingredient of your choice along with the white of the eggs.

4. When the mixture is ready, pour the contents into the air fryer and cook for about 30 minutes over medium temperature.
5. Turn with the aid of a spatula and cook for an additional 5 minutes. Serve and enjoy!

Tuna Omelet

Servings: 4

Total Time: 20 Minutes

Calories: 345

Fat: 18 g

Protein: 6 g

Carbs: 2 g

Fiber: 0.5 g

Ingredients and Quantity

- 2 anchovy fillets
- 8 eggs
- 200 g canned tuna (fat-free)
- 1 tbsp. chopped parsley
- Black pepper, to taste

Direction

1. Cut anchovies into thin strips.
2. Beat eggs, adding anchovies and tuna.
3. Season with parsley and black pepper.
4. Cook the omelet in a lightly oiled air fryer pan at medium temperature.
5. Serve immediately. Enjoy!

Tofu Omelet

Servings: 4

Total Time: 20 Minutes

Calories: 232

Fat: 8 g

Protein: 15 g

Carbs: 3 g

Fiber: 0.8 g

Ingredients and Quantity

- 2 eggs

- 2 tbsp. soy light sauce
- 1 garlic clove, crushed
- 1/2 minced onion
- 400 g chopped tofu
- 1/2 minced green bell pepper
- 1 tbsp. minced parsley
- Black pepper, to taste

Direction

1. In a container, mix eggs with spices.
2. Add the tofu and the peppers. Mix.
3. Pour mixture into an air fryer placed in the air fryer and cook at a low temperature.
4. Sprinkle with parsley before serving. Enjoy!

Smoked Salmon Scrambled Eggs

Servings: 4

Total Time: 20 Minutes

Calories: 200

Fat: 13 g

Protein: 16 g

Carbs: 2 g

Fiber: 1.2 g

Ingredients and Quantity

- 100 g smoked salmon
- 8 eggs
- 80 ml skimmed milk
- 1 tbsp. 0% fat cottage cheese
- 8 chive leaves
- Black pepper and salt

Direction

1. Cut the smoked salmon into thin slices.
2. Beat eggs in a bowl.
3. Season with a little black pepper along with salt.
4. Heat the air fryer with some skimmed milk at the bottom.
5. Mix the eggs and cook at a low temperature, stirring with a spatula.
6. Turn off the heat, add the salmon and cottage cheese.
7. Serve immediately. Garnish with some chive leaves. Serve and enjoy!

Scrambled Eggs

Servings: 2

Total Time: 20 Minutes

Calories: 214

Fat: 13 g

Protein: 11 g

Carbs: 1 g

Fiber: 0.2 g

Ingredients and Quantity

- 4 eggs
- 1/2 liter skimmed milk
- A pinch nutmeg
- 2 sprigs chopped parsley or chives
- Black pepper and salt, to taste

Direction

1. Beat eggs, add milk, then salt along with pepper.
2. Scrape off some nutmeg and cook slowly in the air fryer constantly stirring.
3. Garnish with some parsley or chives and serve immediately. Enjoy!

Tomato Nest

Servings: 4

Total Time: 45 Minutes

Calories: 278

Fat: 16 g

Protein: 20 g

Carbs: 15 g

Fiber: 0.5 g

Ingredients and Quantity

- 8 medium size tomatoes
- 4 eggs
- 200 g low fat ham
- Fresh basil
- Black pepper and salt, to taste

Direction

1. Preheat air fryer for 20 minutes at 220 degrees.
2. Wash the tomatoes. Cut off the top and empty them.
3. Apply seasoning inside the tomatoes with salt and turn them upside down to drain the water.
4. Whisk the eggs, sprinkle black pepper and salt as per your taste and add the ham with a little chopped basil.
5. Spread the mixture over the tomatoes and cook them for 25 to 30 minutes. Serve and enjoy!

Main Dish Recipes

Turkey Breast in Foil

Servings: 4

Total Time: 45 Minutes

Calories: 280

Fat: 9 g

Protein: 18 g

Carbs: 4 g

Fiber: 2.8 g

Ingredients and Quantity

- 4 turkey breasts, 100 g each
- 4 tbsp. mustard
- 4 slices lean ham
- Herb mix
- Black pepper and salt

Direction

1. Preheat air fryer to 180 degrees.
2. Remove fat from turkey breasts if necessary and wrap them in foil on the foil.
3. Grease the turkey breasts with a spoon of mustard, wrap them with a slice of thin ham, and sprinkle with herbs.
4. Add black pepper along with salt. Add a little water, close the foil.
5. Cook for 30 minutes. Serve and enjoy!

Chicken Thighs in Foil

Servings: 2

Total Time: 25 Minutes

Calories: 223

Fat: 11 g

Protein: 24 g

Carbs: 4 g

Fiber: 2.3 g

Ingredients and Quantity

- 100 g 0% fat cottage cheese

- 1 minced shallot
- 1 tbsp. chopped parsley
- 20 chopped chives stalks
- 2 chicken thighs
- Black pepper and salt, to taste

Direction

1. Preheat air fryer to 150 degrees.
2. Prepare the stuffing by mixing cottage cheese, shallot, parsley, and chives. Add black pepper along with salt.
3. Skin the chicken thighs with the help of a sharp knife by cutting a slit about two inches into the thickest part of the meat.
4. Add the stuffing through the slit and coat the chicken thighs with the rest of the total time required to prepare.
5. Cut two sheets of aluminum foil: arrange the thighs in the middle of each sheet and close, making a wrap.
6. Pour some water into the pan and arrange the papers.
7. Cook in the air fryer for 45 minutes. Serve and enjoy!

Cucumber Curry

Servings: 4

Total Time: 42 Minutes

Calories: 150

Fat: 2 g

Protein: 2 g

Carbs: 8 g

Fiber: 1.5 g

Ingredients and Quantity

- 2 medium cucumbers
- 1 small red bell pepper
- 1 small tbsp. curry
- 4 tomatoes
- 100 ml skimmed milk
- 1 tbsp. cornstarch
- Salt, to taste

Direction

1. Cut the cucumbers in two, lengthwise. Then cut the two halves into 1cm sticks.
2. In a non-stick air fryer, sauté the minced pepper with the curry, add the cucumber and simmer for 10 minutes.
3. Add the coarsely sliced tomatoes and cook for another 10 minutes.

4. In another pan, mix the milk with the cornstarch, add to the vegetables and cook for 1 or 2 minutes so that the sauce thickens.
5. Serve it hot. Enjoy!

Tricolor Spinach

Servings: 4

Total Time: 1 Hour 20 Minutes

Calories: 68

Fat: 4 g

Protein: 3 g

Carbs: 4 g

Fiber: 0.6 g

Ingredients and Quantity

- 400 g frozen spinach
- 3 tomatoes
- 2 peppers
- Some thyme stems
- 1 bay leaf
- Black pepper and salt, to taste

Direction

1. Thaw spinach as directed in the total time required to prepare mode.
2. In a saucepan, place the sliced tomatoes, sliced peppers, thyme, bay leaf, and a glass of water.
3. Season adequately using salt along with pepper.
4. Cook for 10 minutes over low heat in an air fryer.
5. Add spinach and serve very hot. Enjoy!

Cooked Eggplant

Servings: 4

Total Time: 1 Hour 20 Minutes

Calories: 31

Fat: 0 g

Protein: 3 g

Carbs: 5 g

Fiber: 0.3 g

Ingredients and Quantity

- 600 g eggplant
- 2 onions
- 1 kg tomatoes, fresh
- 2 garlic cloves
- Black pepper and salt, to taste

Direction

1. Peel the eggplants, cut into 1cm thick slices lengthwise.
2. In a lightly oiled air fryer, sauté the chopped onion at medium temperature.
3. Peel the tomatoes and cut into pieces, add the onion with the peeled and minced garlic cloves.
4. Season adequately using salt along with pepper.
5. Cook for 30 minutes at medium temperature with lid.
6. Mash until mashed and return to air fryer.
7. Add the eggplant to the tomato puree.
8. Cook without lid, slowly, for another 30 minutes.
9. Heat up the spice. Serve and enjoy!

Chicken in Fennel

Servings: 8

Total Time: 1 Hour 25 Minutes

Calories: 243

Fat: 3 g

Protein: 35 g

Carbs: 5 g

Fiber: 2.4 g

Ingredients and Quantity

- 1 1/2 kg chicken scallops
- 2 fresh small onions
- 3 fennel stalks
- A pinch chili powder
- 2 tbsp. fish sauce
- 2 tbsp. soy light sauce
- 2 tbsp. liquid sweetener
- Black pepper and salt

Direction

1. Slice the chicken evenly. Peel the onions and chop.
2. Cut the fennel very thin.
3. In a pan, brown the chicken and cook for 10 minutes with a little oil.
4. Add onions, lemon balm, pepper, fish sauce, soy sauce, sweetener, black pepper along with salt.

5. Reduce the temperature. Cover and cook in the air fryer for 45 minutes. Serve and enjoy!

Meatball with Herbs

Servings: 3

Total Time: 30 Minutes plus 5 Minutes per batch

Calories: 280

Fat: 24 g

Protein: 12 g

Carbs: 6 g

Fiber: 2.8 g

Ingredients and Quantity

- 1 medium onion
- 750 g beef
- 2 garlic cloves
- 1 egg
- 2 tbsp. Chinese plum sauce
- 1 tbsp. Worcestershire sauce
- 2 tbsp. rosemary
- 1 to 2 tbsp. mint or basil
- Black pepper and salt

Direction

1. Mix the chopped onion, ground beef, minced garlic, lightly beaten egg, sauces, and finely chopped herbs.
2. Season adequately using salt along with pepper.
3. Make meatballs the size of a walnut.
4. Cook in small quantities in an air fryer at medium temperature for 5 minutes until evenly browned.
5. Remove excess fat with a paper towel.
6. Serve with tomato sauce. Enjoy!

Marinated Skirt Steak in Coke Zero

Servings: 5

Total Time: 40 Minutes

Calories: 150

Fat: 8 g

Protein: 19 g

Carbs: 1 g

Fiber: 1.5 g

Ingredients and Quantity

- 1 piece steak approximately 1 kg to 1.5 kg or other fat-free meat
- 600 ml to 800 ml Coke Zero
- 10 mini-balls
- Seasoning and salt, to taste

Direction

1. Season the meat with all seasonings to your liking.
2. Put it in a plastic bag and add Coke Zero.
3. Close the plastic bag with a knot so that the soda surrounds all the meat.
4. Place the plastic bag on an air fryer proof dish and marinate in the refrigerator for a few hours.
5. Put the meat in the pressure cooker and seal it to brown.
6. Add Coke Zero and add 100 to 200ml of water if necessary until all meat is covered. Serve and enjoy!

Tandoori Chicken Escallops

Servings: 6

Total Time: 35 Minutes

Calories: 158

Fat: 6 g

Protein: 23 g

Carbs: 2 g

Fiber: 1.5 g

Ingredients and Quantity

- 2 fat-free yogurts
- 2 tsp. tandoori masala (Indian spice)
- 3 cloves garlic, mashed
- 2 cm mashed ginger
- 2 mashed green bell peppers
- Lemon juice
- 6 chicken scallops
- Black pepper and salt, to taste

Direction

1. Mix all ingredients except chicken.
2. Mash the garlic, ginger, and peppers well so that the mixture is homogeneous.
3. Cut the chicken meat so that the mixture penetrates and keep aside to marinate overnight in the refrigerator.
4. The next day, cook for 20 minutes in the air fryer at 180 degrees, then broil to brown. Serve and enjoy!

Codfish

Servings: 8

Total Time: 40 Minutes

Calories: 168

Fat: 5 g

Protein: 26 g

Carbs: 4 g

Fiber: 0.8 g

Ingredients and Quantity

- 2 kg desalted cod loin
- 6 egg whites
- 5 small diced onions
- 2 yellow bell peppers, diced
- 2 red bell peppers, diced
- 2 garlic cloves, crushed
- Cod stock
- 1 cup finely chopped green onions or chives

Direction

1. Cook the cod loins in water for about 30 minutes. Set aside, allow to cool and leave in water.
2. In the air fryer, place the onions, peppers, garlic and the cod stock.
3. When the braised liquid reduces, allow the water to dry completely and add the cod.
4. Adjust the salt, turn off the heat.
5. Beat the egg whites firmly.
6. Assemble the dish with the following layers: Cod, Green onions and egg whites. Serve and enjoy!

Crabs

Servings: 4

Total Time: 35 Minutes

Calories: 128

Fat: 5 g

Protein: 12 g

Carbs: 3 g

Fiber: 1.3 g

Ingredients and Quantity

- 500 g shredded crab meat

- 2 seedless tomatoes
- 1 large onion
- 1 tbsp. light ricotta paste
- 1 tbsp. creamy 0% fat cream cheese
- Parsley, cayenne or Tabasco and salt, to taste

Direction

1. Add the onions and tomatoes to sauté in the air fryer, add crab meat and seasonings and cook.
2. If the meat leaves a lot of water, allow it to dry.
3. When it is cooked, add the ricotta paste and cheese to combine.
4. Cook for 10 minutes and serve. Enjoy!

Crab Broth with Vegetables

Servings: 4

Total Time: 55 Minutes

Calories: 278

Fat: 17 g

Protein: 10 g

Carbs: 12 g

Fiber: 2 g

Ingredients and Quantity

- 12 crabs or crayfish
- 2 peppers, red and green
- 1 large onion
- 1 garlic clove
- 1 medium lemon
- 1/2 bundle cilantro
- 1/2 bundle parsley
- 1 pinch paprika
- 2 chicken broth sachets with 0% fat
- 2 bay leaves
- Salt and pepper, to taste

Direction

1. Clean the crab, cut the peppers and lemon into small pieces, chop the onion, garlic, coriander, and parsley.
2. Pour all ingredients into the air fryer with diluted chicken broth (in 1l of water) and cook for 35 minutes. Serve and enjoy!

Fresh Cod with Herbs

Servings: 4

Total Time: 35 Minutes

Calories: 309

Fat: 8 g

Protein: 49 g

Carbs: 8 g

Fiber: 3 g

Ingredients and Quantity

- 1 shallot
- 1 onion
- 1 bouquet fine herbs
- 4 small peppers
- 1 red bell pepper
- 600 g fresh cod fillet
- 1 lemon
- Black pepper and salt

Direction

1. Preheat air fryer to 210 degrees.
2. Chop the shallots and onion into tiny pieces, then mix with the chopped herbs.
3. Squeeze the lemon juice. Cut the peppers in two. Cut the peppers in four and remove the seeds.
4. Place the fish fillets in four aluminum foil rectangles.
5. Season adequately using salt along with pepper. Then put the bell pepper, a thin layer of herbs, and pepper.
6. Add the lemon juice. Fold the edges of the paper.
7. Cook for 15 minutes. Serve and enjoy!

Fresh Cod with Saffron

Servings: 4

Total Time: 55 Minutes

Calories: 299

Fat: 8 g

Protein: 32 g

Carbs: 10 g

Fiber: 2.8 g

Ingredients and Quantity

- 500 g tomatoes
- 2 garlic cloves, minced
- 100 g leeks
- 100 g minced onion
- 1 sprig fennel
- 3 parsley stems
- 1 pinch saffron
- 4 fresh cod fillets
- 100 ml water
- Black pepper and salt

Direction

1. Cut the tomatoes into pieces.
2. In the air fryer, add garlic, chopped leeks, onions, chopped fennel, parsley, and saffron.
3. Season adequately using salt along with pepper.
4. Cook for 30 minutes. Add fish and cover with water.
5. When it boils, lower the heat and simmer for 10 minutes. Serve and enjoy!

Stuffed Cod

Servings: 4

Total Time: 45 Minutes

Calories: 283

Fat: 7 g

Protein: 33 g

Carbs: 9 g

Fiber: 2.3 g

Ingredients and Quantity

- 50 g oregano
- 25 g chopped white celery
- 1 tbsp. chopped parsley
- 250 ml tomato puree
- 100 g crab meat
- 1 egg
- 800 g cod cut into 8 fillets
- Black pepper and salt

Direction

1. Preheat air fryer to 210 degrees.

2. Using a spatula, combine onion, celery, parsley, tomato puree, crab meat, and egg to make the stuffing. Season it.
3. Spread the stuffing over four fish fillets.
4. Cover with the remaining four fillets.
5. Take the fish with the rest of the tomato juice.
6. Cook for 30 minutes. Serve very hot. Enjoy!

Meat with Eggplants

Servings: 4

Total Time: 30 Minutes

Calories: 336

Fat: 16 g

Protein: 9 g

Carbs: 3 g

Fiber: 3.1 g

Ingredients and Quantity

- 300 g eggplant
- 400 g medium tomatoes
- 1 garlic clove, crushed
- 1 tbsp. minced parsley
- 500 g lean beef, cut into thin strips
- Black pepper and salt, to taste

Direction

1. Peel the eggplants and cut into thin slices.
2. Transfer them to the air fryer and add some salt to release water. Leave for 15 minutes.
3. Put the tomatoes in a pan and wait till it boils. Then cook at medium temperature for 30 minutes.
4. In the bottom of a dish that can be cooked, place half of the vegetables.
5. Season and place the meat on top.
6. Top with the rest of the eggplants and tomatoes.
7. Cook at 210 degrees for 15 minutes. Check seasoning and serve once ready. Enjoy!

Beef with Chilies

Servings: 4

Total Time: 1 Hour 20 Minutes

Calories: 294

Fat: 10 g

Protein: 22 g

Carbs: 9 g

Fiber: 2.5 g

Ingredients and Quantity

- 320 g sirloin
- 4 red bell pepper
- 3 small onions
- 2 tbsp. soy sauce

For the Marinade:

- 1 tbsp. cornstarch
- 4 tbsp. soy sauce

Direction

1. Dip the ribs into very thin strips.
2. Prepare the marinade.
3. Rub the meat in the marinade and refrigerate for 2 hours.
4. Cut the peppers and onions into thin slices.
5. Add to a lightly greased air fryer. Sauté and add a glass of water.
6. Cook over low heat for 30 minutes.
7. When the vegetables are cooked, add the marinated meat, two tablespoons of soy sauce and some water if necessary.
8. Season to taste. Serve and enjoy!

Turkey Medallion

Servings: 4

Total Time: 1 Hour 50 Minutes

Calories: 298

Fat: 16 g

Protein: 51 g

Carbs: 6 g

Fiber: 2.2 g

Ingredients and Quantity

- 100 g mushrooms
- 1 onion
- Parsley
- 4 turkey scallops
- 4 slices non-fat ham
- 500 ml non-fat chicken broth

- 250 ml water
- Black pepper and salt

Direction

1. Wash and clean mushrooms thoroughly and cut with half the onion and parsley.
2. Sauté at medium temperature for 5 to 6 minutes in the air fryer.
3. Season adequately using salt along with pepper.
4. Place a slice of ham in each escalope and then the mushrooms.
5. Wrap the escallops and tie them with a thread.
6. Brown them in air fryer at medium temperature.
7. Roughly cut the rest of the onion. Add broth and water.
8. Season adequately using salt along with pepper.
9. Simmer for 45 minutes, capped. Add the mushroom heads and continue cooking for another 20 minutes.
10. Serve immediately. Enjoy!

Chicken with Lemon and Ginger Curry Sauce

Servings: 5

Total Time: 45 Minutes

Calories: 195

Fat: 16 g

Protein: 34 g

Carbs: 7 g

Fiber: 1.9 g

Ingredients and Quantity

- 4 chicken thighs
- 1 cube fat-free chicken broth
- 1 tarragon stem
- 1 kg funghi
- 1 garlic clove
- 1 packet parsley
- 250 g 0% fat creamy curd
- Black pepper and salt

Direction

1. Brown the chicken legs already seasoned with black pepper along with salt in a lightly oiled pan.
2. Add 100 ml of chicken stock and the well-washed tarragon stem.
3. Wait till it boils, cover, and then lower the heat, letting it cook in the air fryer for 25 minutes.
4. In an air fryer, sauté the washed funghis, the chopped garlic, and the parsley. Season it.
5. At the time of serving, remove the tarragon from the pan and mix the sauce with the curd over low heat. Add the spices.
6. Serve the hot chicken with the braised funghis. Enjoy!

Air Fryer Chicken

Servings: 4

Total Time: 35 Minutes

Calories: 292

Fat: 9 g

Protein: 30 g

Carbs: 9 g

Fiber: 2.3 g

Ingredients and Quantity

- 100 g mushrooms
- 1 garlic clove
- 1 tbsp. coriander
- 1 tsp. black pepper
- 1 L fat free chicken broth
- 250 g cooked chicken breast
- 2 shallots

Direction

1. Cut the mushrooms into slices.
2. Process garlic, coriander, and black pepper until mashed.
3. Place the mushrooms and condiments in a lightly oiled air fryer and sauté the mixture for one minute at medium temperature.
4. Remove from heat and set aside.
5. In a saucepan, boil chicken stock and add the mushrooms and garlic mixture.
6. Cook for 5 minutes with the pan covered.
7. Chop up the chicken into uniform pieces and add to the mixture.
8. Let it cook for a few minutes.
9. Serve with chopped shallots. Enjoy!

Chicken with Gherkin

Servings: 4

Total Time: 50 Minutes

Calories: 135

Fat: 4 g

Protein: 13 g

Carbs: 3 g

Fiber: 1.3 g

Ingredients and Quantity

- 2 large diced chicken breasts
- 500 g cucumber cut thick
- 1 chicken bouillon cube with 0% fat
- 1 green bell pepper, diced
- 1 red bell pepper, diced
- 1 onion, diced
- 1 garlic clove
- 1 bunch cilantro
- 1 tsp. paprika

Direction

1. Scrape the gherkin to remove the thorns and cut into 4 slices.
2. In a pan, fry the chicken in the onion, garlic, and bell peppers for 5 minutes.
3. Add the chicken broth diluted in 500ml of water, the cucumber, the paprika, and the chopped coriander;
4. Cook for 25 minutes over low heat in the air fryer. Serve and enjoy!

Cooked Salmon Escallops with Mustard Sauce

Servings: 4

Total Time: 35 Minutes

Calories: 310

Fat: 10 g

Protein: 40 g

Carbs: 8 g

Fiber: 3.1 g

Ingredients and Quantity

- 4 salmon slices, 200 g each
- 2 shallots
- 1 tbsp. light mustard
- 6 tsp. 0% fat cream cheese
- Chopped dill
- Black pepper and salt, to taste

Direction

1. Place salmon in the freezer for a few minutes, to be able to cut it into thin slices of 50g.
2. In a nonstick air fryer, brown the salmon slices at medium temperature for 1 minute each side. Set aside by keeping warm.
3. Peel and chop the shallots.

4. In the same air fryer, sauté and brown the shallots, top with mustard and cream cheese. Let thicken for 5 minutes over low heat in the air fryer.
5. Put the chopped salmon and dill over the pan again.
6. Serve immediately. Enjoy!

Steamed Sea Bass Fillet with Mint and Cinnamon

Servings: 4

Total Time: 20 Minutes

Calories: 235

Fat: 2 g

Protein: 28 g

Carbs: 4 g

Fiber: 3.1 g

Ingredients and Quantity

- 3 sprigs fresh mint
- 1/2 tsp. ground cinnamon
- 2 cinnamon sticks
- 4 sea bass fillets, with skin
- 10 g coarse salt
- 1/2 lemon, yellow
- Black pepper and salt, to taste

Direction

1. At the bottom of a couscous or steamer, heat the water with fresh mint and cinnamon powder. Save some mint leaves for decoration.
2. Place fish fillets on top of couscous or steaming pan and cook for 10 minutes in the air fryer.
3. Serve the fish seasoned with some lemon juice.
4. Garnish with fresh mint leaves and cinnamon. Enjoy!

Fresh Cod Fillet with Shallots and Mustard

Servings: 2

Total Time: 35 Minutes

Calories: 189

Fat: 14 g

Protein: 14 g

Carbs: 5 g

Fiber: 1.8 g

Ingredients and Quantity

- 4 shallots
- 50 g 0% fat cottage cheese paste
- 1 tbsp. mustard
- 2 tbsp. lemon juice
- 400 g fresh cod fillet
- Black pepper and salt

Direction

1. Preheat air fryer to 180 degrees.
2. Chop the shallots. Put them in a pan with a tablespoon of water and cook until they become translucent.
3. Mix cottage cheese paste with mustard and lemon juice.
4. Season adequately using salt along with pepper.
5. Place the shallot reduction on the bottom of a dish.
6. Arrange the fresh cod over the shallots and pour the cottage sauce.
7. Cook for about 15 minutes. Serve and enjoy!

Indian Style Whiting Fillet

Servings: 2

Total Time: 27 Minutes

Calories: 110

Fat: 2 g

Protein: 17 g

Carbs: 2 g

Fiber: 1.1 g

Ingredients and Quantity

- 1 sachet nonfat fish broth
- 300 g sea bass fillet
- 1 medium onion
- 1 egg yolk
- 1/2 tsp. curry powder
- A pinch saffron
- 1 tbsp. chopped parsley
- Salt and pepper, to taste

Direction

1. Boil 250ml of water with the fish stock.
2. Cook the whiting fillets for about 5 minutes.
3. Meanwhile, peel the onion by browning it in a lightly oiled air fryer.

4. Throw the fish stock over and let it reduce for 2 minutes.
5. Add the egg yolk diluted in a little liquid. Let it thicken slowly.
6. Season it. Add curry powder and saffron.
7. Arrange the sea bass fillets on a hot plate and pour the sauce.
8. Sprinkle with the chopped parsley. Serve and enjoy!

Halibut Fillet

Servings: 1

Total Time: 12 Minutes

Calories: 125

Fat: 2 g

Protein: 19 g

Carbs: 2 g

Fiber: 1.2 g

Ingredients and Quantity

- 200 g halibut fillet
- 1 fresh tomato
- 1 minced garlic clove
- Some capers
- 4 basil leaves

Direction

1. Place the halibut fillet in an air fryer dish. In another dish, combine mashed tomatoes, garlic, capers, and basil.
2. Cover the fish fillet with this mixture and cover.
3. Cook in the air fryer for 2 minutes over high heat. Enjoy!

Fillet of Sole with Sorrel

Servings: 2

Total Time: 24 Minutes

Calories: 75

Fat: 2 g

Protein: 13 g

Carbs: 1 g

Fiber: 0.7 g

Ingredients and Quantity

- 4 sole fillets
- 2 squeezed lemons
- 10 chopped sorrel leaves
- Black pepper and salt, to taste

Direction

1. Wash and dry the fish fillets.
2. Let them marinate for at least 2 hours in lemon juice and chopped sorrel. Drain.
3. In a nonstick air fryer, broil both sides of the marinated fillets.
4. Season adequately using salt along with pepper.
5. Serve the steaks with the marinade sauce. Enjoy!

Fresh Codfish with Curry

Servings: 4

Total Time: 50 Minutes

Calories: 151

Fat: 2 g

Protein: 27 g

Carbs: 7 g

Fiber: 1.5 g

Ingredients and Quantity

- 700 g fresh cod
- 1 onion
- 3 garlic cloves
- 4 dried peppers
- 4 rocotillo peppers
- 1 tsp. coriander seeds
- 1 tsp. turmeric
- 1 tsp. cumin
- 500 g tomatoes
- 4 tbsp. water
- 3 tbsp. lemon juice
- Salt and pepper, to taste

Direction

1. Prepare fish by removing thorns, washing, and dicing.
2. Chop the onion and mash the garlic, chop the peppers and sauté in a nonstick air fryer, lightly oiled.
3. Add seasonings and cook for 5 minutes.
4. Add the crushed tomatoes as well as the water and lemon juice. Wait till it boils.
5. Reduce heat and simmer for 15 minutes without lid.

6. Then add the fish cubes. Sprinkle black pepper and salt as per your taste and continue cooking for 10 minutes over low heat. Serve and enjoy!

Tandoori Chicken

Servings: 4

Total Time: 1 Hour 5 Minutes

Calories: 220

Fat: 5 g

Protein: 8 g

Carbs: 4 g

Fiber: 2.2 g

Ingredients and Quantity

- 4 chicken thighs
- 1 lemon juice
- 4 tbsp. tandoori curry paste
- Two 0% fat yogurt
- 1 garlic clove
- Black pepper and salt, to taste

Direction

1. Remove skin from chicken thighs and split the two in the joint.
2. Make several cuts in the meat.
3. Arrange the chicken pieces in a deep dish. Add the lemon juice.
4. In a large bowl, combine tandoori curry paste, yogurt, and mashed garlic clove.
5. Add black pepper along with salt. Pour the mixture over the chicken.
6. Cover. Marinate at least six hours in the refrigerator, turning the pieces into the marinade two to three times.
7. Remove chicken thighs from marinade.
8. Drain and arrange over the air fryer rack, cooking for 35 minutes and turning the pieces over the remaining marinade three to four times. Serve and enjoy!

Chicken in Lemon Crust

Servings: 2

Total Time: 1 Hour 15 Minutes

Calories: 220

Fat: 7 g

Protein: 58 g

Carbs: 10 g

Fiber: 2 g

Ingredients and Quantity

- 1 bundle herbs
- 2 green lemons
- 1 onion
- One 400 g to 500 g chicken
- 2 egg whites
- 2 kg coarse salt
- Black pepper and salt, to taste

Direction

1. The day before put the bundle of herbs, the half lemon juice, a peeled onion cut into pieces, and the chicken to marinate in a liter of water.
2. The next day, stuff the chicken inside with the marinade spices.
3. Mix egg whites with coarse salt and cover a pan with this total time required to prepare.
4. Put the chicken in the middle of the pan and cover it with the remaining salt.
5. Cook for 50 minutes at 210 degrees.
6. To serve, break the salt crust with a spoon, cut the chicken in two, and drizzle with the lemon juice. Enjoy!

Side Dish Recipes

Marinated Chicken Skewers

Servings: 4

Total Time: 40 Minutes

Calories: 130

Fat: 4 g

Protein: 24 g

Carbs: 4 g

Fiber: 1.7 g

Ingredients and Quantity

- 4 chicken breasts
- 4 garlic cloves
- 2 lemons
- 1 tsp. cumin powder
- 1 tsp. thyme
- 1 green or red bell pepper
- 8 onions
- Salt and pepper, to taste

Direction

1. The day before, cut the chicken breasts into pieces, place them on a deep plate with the minced garlic, lemon juice, cumin, thyme, black pepper along with salt.
2. Cover with film paper and marinate in the refrigerator until the next day.
3. Dice the bell pepper and peeled onions, then prepare the skewers, interspersing the chicken and vegetables.
4. Brush the sauce and cook on the air fryer grill for 5 minutes each side. Serve and enjoy!

Chicken with Lemon and Cherry Tomatoes

Servings: 2

Total Time: 60 Minutes

Calories: 240

Fat: 11 g

Protein: 31 g

Carbs: 5 g

Fiber: 2.4 g

Ingredients and Quantity

- 5 thyme sprigs
- 2 chickens
- 1 lemon
- 500 ml nonfat chicken broth
- 2 medium onions
- 2 garlic cloves
- 700 g cherry tomatoes
- Black pepper and salt

Direction

1. Remove the thyme leaves. Shred the chickens in a dish to be cooked.
2. Cover them with the lemon wedges.
3. Cook in air fryer for 20 minutes at 180 degrees.
4. Halfway through cooking, drizzle chicken with chicken stock.
5. Chop the onions and cut the garlic.
6. Take the dish out of the air fryer.
7. Distribute the onions, tomatoes, and garlic among the chickens.
8. Season adequately using salt along with pepper.
9. Mix everything to cover the tomatoes.
10. Cook in air fryer again for another 20 minutes. Serve and enjoy!

Turkey Thighs with Chilies

Servings: 4

Total Time: 1 Hour 10 Minutes

Calories: 190

Fat: 10 g

Protein: 20 g

Carbs: 1 g

Fiber: 1.9 g

Ingredients and Quantity

- 2 turkey thighs
- 3 red bell peppers
- 50 ml wine vinegar
- 2 tbsp. 0% fat creamy curd
- Black pepper and salt, to taste

Direction

1. Brown the turkey thighs in a non-stick air fryer with a little water and cook in air fryer for 40 minutes over low heat, stirring regularly.
2. Cook the peppers in boiling water, then peel and remove the seeds.
3. Cut into pieces and beat in a blender to turn into syrup.
4. Remove the thighs from the pan and add the vinegar.
5. Add the curd, chili sauce, black pepper along with salt, and wait till it boils.
6. Put the thighs on a plate and drizzle with the sauce. Serve and enjoy!

Stuffed Chicken Breast

Servings: 5

Total Time: 35 Minutes

Calories: 240

Fat: 15 g

Protein: 22 g

Carbs: 6 g

Fiber: 2.4 g

Ingredients and Quantity

- 10 thinly slice chicken breast fillets
- 3 tbsp. soy light
- 350 ml Coke Zero
- 1 onion
- Freshly grated ginger
- Garlic
- Salt, to taste
- 1 packet spinach
- 300 g light ricotta
- 2 tbsp. 0% fat creamy curd

Direction

1. Let chicken fillets marinate in light soy sauce and Coke for about 2 hours.
2. Sauté spinach, add ricotta and curd.
3. Fill the fillets with the spinach cream, roll up, and secure the ends with sticks.
4. Put in an air fryer proof dish, cook with soy sauce.
5. Cover with aluminum foil so as not to dry and cook for about 15 minutes.
6. Remove the aluminum foil and leave gild.
7. Serve with creamy spinach cream. Enjoy!

Rolls of Smoked Salmon

Servings: 3

Sussy Fisch

Total Time: 10 Minutes plus 40 Minutes per Omelet

Calories: 200

Fat: 5 g

Protein: 8 g

Carbs: 8 g

Fiber: 2 g

Ingredients and Quantity

- 3 eggs
- 3 tbsp. water
- 3 tbsp. cornstarch
- 250 g 0% fat cottage cheese
- 2 tbsp. minced chives
- 1 tbsp. minced ginger
- 100 g smoked salmon
- Some parsley leaves
- Black pepper, to taste

Direction

1. Mix an egg, a tablespoon of water, a teaspoon of cornstarch and make a thin omelet in an air fryer.
2. Repeat the operation with the rest of the eggs, water, and cornstarch.
3. Spread cottage cheese gently on each omelet, sprinkle with chives, and ginger.
4. Distribute the salmon and add black pepper. Roll up the omelets, squeezing tightly on a movie paper.
5. Store in the freezer for three hours.
6. Cut into slices with a sharp knife and serve on a plate decorated with parsley. Enjoy!

Braid of Sole and Salmon

Servings: 4

Total Time: 60 Minutes

Calories: 140

Fat: 7 g

Protein: 22 g

Carbs: 2 g

Fiber: 1.4 g

Ingredients and Quantity

- 4 thinly sliced sole fillets
- 2 fresh salmon fillets
- Freshly grated ginger

- 2 tbsp. soy light
- 250 ml water
- 1 grated onion
- Lemon juice drops
- Salt, to taste

Direction

1. Season the fish with onion, lemon drops, and salt and set aside.
2. Make a mixture of soy sauce with water and grated ginger and marinate.
3. Cut the fish into strips. Using two strips of sole and one of salmon, braid and secure the ends with wooden sticks.
4. Put in an air fryer proof dish and drizzle with soy sauce and ginger.
5. Cook covered with baking paper or aluminum for cooking.
6. Remove the paper to finish cooking. Serve and enjoy!

Curried Boiled Eggs

Servings: 1

Total Time: 20 Minutes

Calories: 198

Fat: 16 g

Protein: 13 g

Carbs: 5 g

Fiber: 1.9 g

Ingredients and Quantity

- 1/2 onion
- 8 tbsp. skim milk
- A pinch cornstarch
- 1 tsp. curry
- 2 boiled eggs
- Black pepper and salt, to taste

Direction

1. In an air fryer, cook the onion with half the milk for 10 minutes at medium temperature, stirring continuously.
2. Add the cornstarch and the remaining milk, stirring vigorously. Add Black pepper and salt and curry.
3. Cut the boiled eggs into slices and arrange them on a plate.
4. Pour the sauce over the eggs. Serve and enjoy!

Chicken Curry and Yogurt Escallops

Servings: 4

Total Time: 10 Minutes

Calories: 250

Fat: 20 g

Protein: 32 g

Carbs: 5 g

Fiber: 2.5 g

Ingredients and Quantity

- 25 g nonfat natural yogurt
- 3 tbsp. curry
- 4 chicken escallops
- Black pepper and salt, to taste

Direction

1. Prepare the barbecue embers.
2. Mix together yogurts, Black pepper and salt, and curry powder.
3. Marinate the escallops for 2 hours in the refrigerator.
4. Grill the escallops for 5 minutes in an air fryer by dipping them once or twice in the marinade during cooking. Serve and enjoy!

Crispy Chicken Wings

Servings: 2

Total Time: 30 Minutes

Calories: 100

Fat: 5 g

Protein: 15 g

Carbs: 5 g

Fiber: 1 g

Ingredients and Quantity

- 3 pairs chicken wings
- 1 small cup light soy sauce
- 1 garlic clove, mashed
- 1 tbsp. liquid sweetener
- 4 tsp. condiments (cloves, peppers, cinnamon, fennel and star anise)
- 1 tsp. chopped fresh ginger

Direction

1. Mix all ingredients in a container.
2. Marinate for two to three hours, stirring occasionally.
3. Place in the air fryer in a pan to bake and cook.
4. When the chicken wings begin to brown (in 5-10 minutes).
5. Turn them over and let them cook for another 5-10 minutes. Serve and enjoy!

Chicken with Lemon

Servings: 4

Total Time: 60 Minutes

Calories: 225

Fat: 3 g

Protein: 19 g

Carbs: 3 g

Fiber: 2.3 g

Ingredients and Quantity

- 500 g chicken
- 1 chopped onion
- 2 garlic cloves
- 1/2 tsp. ground ginger
- Juice and zest of 2 lemons
- 2 spoons soy light sauce
- 1 bundle herbs
- 1/4 tsp. cinnamon powder
- 1/4 tsp. ginger powder
- Black pepper and salt, to taste

Direction

1. Cut the chicken into medium-sized cubes.
2. In a nonstick coating pan, sauté the onion, garlic, and ginger in the air fryer at medium temperature for 3 or 4 minutes.
3. Add chicken and cook over high heat for 2 minutes, stirring with a spatula.
4. Add lemon juice, soy sauce, and 150ml of water.
5. Add bundle of herbs, cinnamon, ginger powder, and lemon zest.
6. Sprinkle black pepper and salt as per your taste and cook in the air fryer for 45 minutes.
7. Serve very hot. Enjoy!

Salmon Fillets with Mint

Servings: 2

Total Time: 50 Minutes

Calories: 238

Fat: 17 g

Protein: 26 g

Carbs: 5 g

Fiber: 1.5 g

Ingredients and Quantity

- 500 g fresh salmon fillet
- 2 to 3 tbsp. fresh mint
- 1 large zucchini
- 1 slice smoked salmon
- 2 jelly sheets
- 1 tbsp. 0% fat cottage cheese
- Black pepper and salt

Direction

1. Cook the fresh salmon fillet in the wrapper in the air fryer for 30 minutes or in the steam wrapped in foil.
2. Let it cool. Wash and chop the fresh mint.
3. Wash the zucchini and cut into thin slices lengthwise, keeping the peel.
4. Quickly brown the zucchini slices in a nonstick air fryer over high heat with a little oil. Let cool.
5. Roughly shred the cooked salmon and chop the smoked salmon. In a saucepan, add previously softened gelatin leaves to cold water and already drained.
6. Add the cottage cheese and mint to the salmon.
7. Mix everything and sprinkle black pepper and salt as per your taste.
8. Fill four jars with the zucchini slices and add the salmon mixture.
9. Leave 12 hours in the refrigerator and remove 30 minutes before serving. Enjoy!

Kani and Shrimp Fry with Champignon

Servings: 4

Total Time: 33 Minutes

Calories: 250

Fat: 12 g

Protein: 35 g

Carbs: 10 g

Fiber: 2.5 g

Ingredients and Quantity

- 2 garlic cloves
- 1 packet parsley
- 500 g mushrooms
- 500 g Kani
- 500 g prawns

Direction

1. Chop the garlic and parsley at the same time and set aside.
2. Wash the mushrooms, drain and chop them. Reserve.
3. Cut the Kani sticks into cubes.
4. Peel the prawns and cut into cubes.
5. In a nonstick air fryer, sauté the shrimps in the air fryer and then the mushrooms.
6. Let the water evaporate for one minute.
7. Then add the Kanis. Season and add garlic and parsley mixture and serve immediately. Enjoy!

Fish in the Paper

Servings: 4

Total Time: 30 Minutes

Calories: 175

Fat: 6 g

Protein: 6 g

Carbs: 8 g

Fiber: 1.7 g

Ingredients and Quantity

- 2 onions
- 2 tomatoes
- 2 carrots
- 1 green bell pepper
- 2 sprigs celery
- 2 sprigs parsley
- 4 slices lean fish
- Black pepper and salt

Direction

1. Preheat air fryer to 250 degrees.
2. Chop the onions, tomatoes, carrots, peppers, celery, and parsley.
3. Season adequately using salt along with pepper.
4. Wash and dry the fish. On a sheet of parchment paper, place the fish and chopped vegetables.

5. Close the papers tightly and cook at 180 degrees. Serve and enjoy!

Quiche with Tuna and Tomato Paste

Servings: 3

Total Time: 40 Minutes

Calories: 175

Fat: 7 g

Protein: 24 g

Carbs: 5 g

Fiber: 1.6 g

Ingredients and Quantity

- 2 eggs
- 4 egg whites
- 2 small tomatoes
- 1 can natural tuna
- 2 tbsp. 0% fat cottage cheese
- 2 pinches fine herbs
- Black pepper and salt, to taste

Direction

1. Make an omelet in a lightly oiled dish in the air fryer.
2. Cut the tomatoes into thin slices, shred the tuna and add the cottage cheese and herbs.
3. Mix all ingredients and place in a dish that can be cooked.
4. Cook for 20 to 25 minutes at 180 degrees. Serve and enjoy!

Fish Pots with Tomato Sauce

Servings: 2

Total Time: 50 Minutes

Calories: 195

Fat: 2 g

Protein: 14 g

Carbs: 3 g

Fiber: 1.9 g

Ingredients and Quantity

- 400 g sole fillet

- 1 packet parsley
- 1 egg
- 2 tbsp. 0% fat curd
- 800 g fresh tomatoes
- 1 pinch thyme
- 1 bay leaf
- 1 garlic clove
- 1 shallot
- Black pepper and salt

Direction

1. Shred two halibut fillets, sprinkle black pepper and salt as per your taste, add parsley.
2. Beat one egg and add two tablespoons of curd.
3. Distribute in two lightly oiled cups and cook in air fryer for 20 to 25 minutes at medium temperature (180 degrees).
4. Wait a few minutes before unmolding.
5. In the meantime, prepare the sauce with 800g peeled tomatoes, cooked for about 15 minutes and blended with thyme, bay leaf, garlic clove, and chopped shallot.
6. Cover the fish with the sauce at the time of serving. Enjoy!

Vegetable Pudding

Servings: 2

Total Time: 25 Minutes

Calories: 95

Fat: 0 g

Protein: 2 g

Carbs: 10 g

Fiber: 0.9 g

Ingredients and Quantity

- 4 eggs
- 1 pinch nutmeg
- 500 ml skimmed milk
- 1 tbsp. finely chopped herbs
- 200 g chopped vegetables (tomato, zucchini, broccoli, eggplant, carrot)
- Black pepper and salt, to taste

Direction

1. Beat egg with the spices and add the warm milk.
2. Add the vegetables and cook in 180 degree air fryer for 15 minutes. Serve and enjoy!

Eggplant Pudding

Servings: 2

Total Time: 50 Minutes

Calories: 135

Fat: 6 g

Protein: 5 g

Carbs: 8 g

Fiber: 0.9 g

Ingredients and Quantity

- 400 g eggplant
- 3 eggs
- 200 ml skimmed milk
- Nutmeg
- Some thyme stems
- Some rosemary stems
- Black pepper and salt

Direction

1. Wash and peel the eggplants, cut into slices and set aside in a colander.
2. Let it pour for 30 minutes by adding a little salt.
3. Dry the slices before cooking in boiling water for 5 minutes and then drain again.
4. Preheat air fryer to 150 degrees.
5. Make an omelet and season.
6. Mix in milk and scrape off some of the nutmeg. Sprinkle thyme and rosemary.
7. In a baking form, arrange eggplant slices and pour egg mixture with milk on top.
8. Cook for 30 minutes. Serve and enjoy!

Mushroom Soufflé

Servings: 1

Total Time: 25 Minutes

Calories: 239

Fat: 6 g

Protein: 17 g

Carbs: 5 g

Fiber: 2.3 g

Ingredients and Quantity

- 150 g mushrooms
- 1 whole egg plus 1 egg white
- 3 tbsp. curd with 0% fat
- Black pepper and salt, to taste

Direction

1. Preheat air fryer to 180 degrees.
2. Dip the mushrooms for 2 minutes in a pan full of boiling water. Then mash them in a blender.
3. Mix the shredded mushrooms with the egg yolk, the curd, and the two beaten egg whites.
4. Season with Black pepper and salt and transfer to a small pot.
5. Cook for about 10 minutes. Serve and enjoy!

Cucumber Soufflé with Basil

Servings: 1

Total Time: 35 Minutes

Calories: 125

Fat: 10 g

Protein: 10 g

Carbs: 3 g

Fiber: 1.2 g

Ingredients and Quantity

- 1/2 cucumber
- 4 tbsp. 0% fat cottage cheese
- 1/2 packet fresh basil
- 6 egg whites
- 4 tomatoes
- 2 onions
- Black pepper and salt

Direction

1. Grind cucumber in a blender and stir in cottage cheese. Season adequately using salt along with pepper.
2. Chop eight basil leaves and add to the total time required to prepare.
3. Beat the egg whites with snow and incorporate them in the cucumber and cottage cheese mixture.
4. Peel and remove the seeds from the tomatoes. Cut the tomatoes into cubes.
5. Chop the onions and sauté for a few minutes in air fryer on medium heat, dry.
6. Add tomatoes, season and simmer for 15 minutes. Lightly grease a few individual pots.
7. Put a spoonful of tomato and onion sauce in the bottom of each pot, and then fill two-thirds of the pot with the soufflé mixture.
8. Cook in air fryer for 15 minutes at 200 degrees.
9. When the soufflés are cooked, put a basil leaf in each pot to decorate. Serve and enjoy!

Chicken Liver with Herbs

Servings: 4

Total Time: 50 Minutes

Calories: 172

Fat: 6 g

Protein: 21 g

Carbs: 1 g

Fiber: 1.7 g

Ingredients and Quantity

- 600 g chicken liver
- 1 minced onion
- 1 minced garlic clove
- 1/2 packet parsley
- 1/2 packet cilantro
- Pepper and salt, to taste
- Bundle of herbs (thyme and bay leaf)
- 1 tbsp. sunflower oil
- 1 cube 0% fat chicken broth

Direction

1. Mix and let chicken liver marinate with chopped onions and garlic, a pinch of pepper, salt, and a bundle of herbs for 10 minutes.
2. Dilute the chicken stock cube in 500ml of hot water.
3. Sauté the mixture with a tablespoon of sunflower oil and add the diluted chicken broth.
4. Cook in air fryer for 30 minutes.
5. Add coriander and parsley to the end. Serve and enjoy!

Chicken Heart Skewers with Herbs

Servings: 4

Total Time: 35 Minutes

Calories: 153

Fat: 9 g

Protein: 16 g

Carbs: 1 g

Fiber: 1.5 g

Ingredients and Quantity

- 500 g chicken heart
- 1 minced onion
- 1 minced garlic clove
- Salt and pepper, to taste
- Herbs (rosemary, fennel, basil, thyme and lavender)
- 1 red bell pepper
- 1 green bell pepper
- 16 wooden skewers

Direction

1. Marinate Chicken heart in garlic, herbs, salt along with pepper for 10 minutes.
2. Cut the onion and bell pepper into large squares.
3. Make skewers of chicken hearts with peppers and onions (1 chicken heart, 1 onion, 1 bell pepper (red), 1 bell pepper (green). Repeat 3 times).
4. Cook in air fryer for 10 minutes. Serve and enjoy!

Tarragon Chicken Terrine

Servings: 6

Total Time: 2 Hours 10 Minutes

Calories: 327

Fat: 17 g

Protein: 18 g

Carbs: 4 g

Fiber: 3.2 g

Ingredients and Quantity

- 2 leaks
- 2 carrots
- 2 garlic cloves
- 1 chicken tied with twine
- 2 gelatin sheets
- 500 ml fat free broth
- 1 onion
- 1 packet tarragon
- 200 g chicken liver
- Salt and pepper, to taste

Direction

Note: This recipe should be prepared the day before.

1. Wash the leeks and peel the carrots and garlic.

2. Put the chicken in a pan, add the broth, and cover with cold water.
3. Add the prepared vegetables, the onion, some tarragon stems, black pepper along with salt.
4. Wait till it boils, cover and simmer for 1 hour and 30 minutes in air fryer, stirring regularly.
5. Halfway through cooking, add chicken liver without nerves.
6. When cooking is done, cut chicken and liver into large cubes.
7. Halve broth and filter. Add the gelatin leaves previously soaked in cold water and drained.
8. Place the tarragon leaves in the bottom of a pot and drizzle with a little broth.
9. Make successive layers with half the chicken and liver cubes, the carrots, and the rest of the chicken. Drizzle with chicken stock.
10. Refrigerate for 24 hours. Serve and enjoy!

Leak Turkey Breast

Servings: 4

Total Time: 50 Minutes

Calories: 220

Fat: 8 g

Protein: 25 g

Carbs: 3 g

Fiber: 2.2 g

Ingredients and Quantity

- 800 g leek, white
- 200 g turkey breast
- 1 shallot
- 2 eggs
- 90 g creamy curd with 0% fat
- Salt

Direction

1. Cut the leek into small pieces and steam for 10 minutes.
2. Sauté minced shallot and turkey breast in a frying pan.
3. Beat eggs with cream cheese and salt. Mix the leeks and braised turkey breast with the shallot.
4. Transfer to a lightly oiled form of oil.
5. On top, put the egg and curd mixture.
6. Cook in air fryer for 20 minutes at 150 degrees. Serve and enjoy!

Smoked Chicken Patties

Servings: 2

Total Time: 1 Hour 5 Minutes

Calories: 150

Fat: 9 g

Protein: 20 g

Carbs: 3 g

Fiber: 1.5 g

Ingredients and Quantity

- 7 egg whites
- 60 ml water
- 1 tbsp. cornstarch
- 175 g smoked chicken breast
- 200 g minced mushrooms
- 2 minced onions
- 2 tbsp. 0% fat cottage cheese
- 1 tbsp. chopped chives
- 20 boiled chives stalks in water, to make them flexible
- Black pepper and salt, to taste

Direction

1. Mix egg whites, water, and cornstarch.
2. Heat a nonstick air fryer in air fryer and cook the spoon-to-spoon mixture to get 20 round pies 10cm in diameter.
3. Wipe off excess water with a paper towel and let cool room temperature.
4. In medium heat in the air fryer, sauté the chopped chicken, mushrooms, and chopped onions in a lightly oiled frying pan.
5. Lower the heat and add the cottage cheese, sprinkle with the chives and sprinkle black pepper and salt as per your taste.
6. Divide the stuffing between the 20 pies and close in a pie shape with the help of the chive stalks.
7. Store in a cool place and serve at room temperature. Enjoy!

Tikka Skewers

Servings: 4

Total Time: 35 Minutes

Calories: 178

Fat: 4 g

Protein: 13 g

Carbs: 5 g

Fiber: 1.5 g

Ingredients and Quantity

- 800 g chicken breast
- 1 onion
- 1 garlic clove
- 20 g fresh ginger
- 2 tbsp. lemon juice
- 100 ml 0% fat yogurt
- 1/2 tbsp. coriander powder
- 1/2 tbsp. cumin powder
- 1 tsp. garam masala (Indian spice)
- 2 tbsp. chopped coriander
- Black pepper and salt, to taste

Direction

1. Cut chicken breasts into 2cm strips.
2. Peel the onion and garlic and reduce the puree in a blender.
3. Add the peeled and grated ginger, lemon juice, salt, yogurt, all spices, and coriander. Then mix.
4. Let the chicken pieces and the sauce marinade for 2 hours in the refrigerator.
5. Put the chicken pieces on wooden skewers. Cook for 8 to 10 minutes on the air fryer grill, turning regularly.
6. Serve hot, accompanied by cucumber, fresh onions, and lemon. Enjoy!

Dinner Recipes

Raspberry Pudding with Goji Berry

Servings: 6

Total Time: 10 Minutes

Calories: 170

Fat: 9 g

Protein: 5 g

Carbs: 10 g

Fiber: 1.7 g

Ingredients and Quantity

- 600 ml skimmed milk
- 2 tbsp. skimmed milk powder
- 2 boxes zero sugar raspberry flavored gelatin
- 200 ml cold skimmed milk
- 4 tbsp. Goji Berry

Direction

1. Soak the goji berries in 200ml cold milk to hydrate.
2. In a pan, put the 600ml of milk and dissolve the gelatin in the air fryer when the milk is hot.
3. Add the two tablespoons of milk powder and 200ml of cold milk (without goji berries).
4. Beat in mixer until foam is obtained. Put some goji berries into the bottom of a pudding pan and pour the milk and gelatin mixture.
5. Take the rest of the gojis and go gently.
6. Refrigerate for 2 hours to harden.
7. Remove the pan from the refrigerator and place it in a dish with boiling water.
8. Rotate the pan so the pudding will come loose from the sides and make the syrup. Serve and enjoy!

Coffee Cream

Servings: 4

Total Time: 25 Minutes

Calories: 50

Fat: 5 g

Protein: 0 g

Carbs: 1 g

Fiber: 0.5 g

Ingredients and Quantity

- 600 ml skimmed milk
- 1 tsp. coffee extract or ground coffee
- 2 eggs
- 2 tbsp. sweetener

Direction

1. Boil the milk in an air fryer and coffee extract.
2. Whisk the eggs with the sweetener and incorporate it in the milk and coffee mixture, stirring constantly.
3. Distribute the mixture in pots and cook in a water bath for 20 minutes in the air fryer heated to 140 degrees.
4. Serve cold. Enjoy!

Spice Cream

Total Time: 40 Minutes

Calories: 50

Fat: 5 g

Protein: 0 g

Carbs: 1 g

Fiber: 0.5 g

Ingredients and Quantity

- 250 ml skimmed milk
- 1 vanilla bean
- 1/2 tsp. ground cinnamon
- 1 clove
- 1 star anise
- 2 egg yolks
- 2 tbsp. sweetener
- 200 g creamy curd with 0% fat milk

Direction

1. Cut vanilla into two lengthwise, cinnamon, cloves, and anise in a pan and wait till it boils.
2. In a bowl, beat the egg yolks with the sweetener until the dough is light.
3. Pour the warm milk slowly over the egg yolks, stirring constantly.
4. Put the total time required to prepare in a pan and cook in air fryer for 12 minutes over low heat, stirring frequently, until the cream begins to be consistent.
5. Sift the cream and let cool.
6. Incorporate the curd into the cold cream.
7. Refrigerate. Serve cold. Enjoy!

Vanilla Cream

Servings: 5

Total Time: 30 Minutes

Calories: 50

Fat: 5 g

Protein: 0 g

Carbs: 1 g

Fiber: 0.5 g

Ingredients and Quantity

- 110 ml skim milk
- 100 g culinary sweetener
- 1 vanilla bean
- 3 egg yolks
- 1 egg white

Direction

1. Boil milk and vanilla.
2. Remove from heat and let cool, remove vanilla and add culinary sweetener.
3. Add the already cold milk, the yolks and the white.
4. Mix and transfer to a pot.
5. The cream will harden by cooking in a double boiler in the air fryer for 20 minutes. Serve and enjoy!

Snow Eggs

Servings: 2

Total Time: 30 Minutes

Calories: 70

Fat: 5 g

Protein: 6 g

Carbs: 1 g

Fiber: 0.7 g

Ingredients and Quantity

- 250 ml skimmed milk
- 2 eggs
- 1 tbsp. liquid sweetener

Direction

1. Boil the milk. Beat the egg yolks and add the sweetener.
2. Gradually incorporate into boiled milk.
3. Heat over low heat in air fryer, stirring constantly with a wooden spoon and scraping the bottom well.
4. As soon as the cream thickens, remove the pan from the air fryer. Do not let it boil as the cream can get very liquid.
5. Then beat the egg whites until they are firm.
6. With a tablespoon, make snowballs and place them in a pan of boiling water.
7. As soon as the egg whites swell, remove with a slotted spoon and drain on a dishtowel.
8. When the yolk cream is cold, add the egg whites and serve. Enjoy!

Milk Eggs

Servings: 2

Total Time: 50 Minutes

Calories: 70

Fat: 5 g

Protein: 6 g

Carbs: 1 g

Fiber: 0.7 g

Ingredients and Quantity

- 500 ml skim milk
- 60 g liquid sweetener
- 1 vanilla bean
- 4 eggs

Direction

1. Boil the milk with the sweetener and vanilla, previously cut in two, lengthwise, and without the seeds.
2. In a bowl, beat eggs to form an omelet.
3. Remove the vanilla from the milk and gradually add the warm milk over the beaten eggs, stirring constantly.
4. Transfer the mixture to an air fryer-safe dish and cook for 40 minutes in a double boiler, in the air fryer preheated to 220 degrees.
5. Serve cold. Enjoy!

Snack Recipes

Golden Fillet with Shallot Compote

Servings: 1

Total Time: 35 Minutes

Calories: 203

Fat: 9 g

Protein: 23 g

Carbs: 5 g

Fiber: 2 g

Ingredients and Quantity

- 1 small shallot
- 2 golden fillets
- 1 tbsp. chopped parsley
- Black pepper and salt

Direction

1. Peel and chop the shallot.
2. Cook it over low heat in a lightly oiled nonstick frying pan. The shallot shall not brown.
3. Pre-heat the air fryer at 180 °.
4. On two sheets of parchment paper, spread the shallot and place a golden filet on top of each sheet.
5. Add Black pepper and salt and sprinkle parsley.
6. Close the wrappers and place them in an air fryer proof dish for about 15 minutes. Serve and enjoy!

Shimeji and Shitake Quiche

Servings: 4

Total Time: 1 Hour 15 Minutes

Calories: 246

Fat: 12 g

Protein: 18 g

Carbs: 5 g

Fiber: 2.4 g

Ingredients and Quantity

- 3 egg yolks

- 4 egg whites
- 1 small tray of shimeji
- 1 small tray of shitake
- 200 ml skimmed milk
- 4 tbsp. light ricotta
- 2 tbsp. creamy curd with 0% fat
- Salt, onion, garlic and herbs, to taste

Direction

1. Wash the shimejis and shitakes well and cook in water.
2. Cut into pieces and sauté with onion, garlic, salt and spices.
3. Lastly, add the cream cheese.
4. Beat the egg yolks, ricotta and milk in a blender.
5. Put this mixture into the shimejis and sautéed shitakes.
6. Beat the egg whites and mix gently.
7. Pour the batter into a removable bottom pan.
8. Cook in the air fryer at 160 degrees until golden brown. Serve and enjoy!

Steamed Cauliflower

Servings: 2

Total Time: 25 Minutes

Calories: 25

Fat: 0 g

Protein: 3 g

Carbs: 5 g

Fiber: 0.2 g

Ingredients and Quantity

- 400 g cauliflower
- 2 boiled eggs
- Lemon juice
- 2 tsp. chopped parsley
- 1 pinch cumin
- Black pepper and salt, to taste

Direction

1. Steam the cauliflower in the air fryer for 15 minutes.
2. Put it on a plate and cover it with the shredded boiled eggs in a mixer.
3. Season with lemon juice, parsley, cumin, black pepper along with salt. Serve and enjoy!

Zucchini with Tomato Sauce

Servings: 2

Total Time: 50 Minutes

Calories: 110

Fat: 6 g

Protein: 9 g

Carbs: 5 g

Fiber: 0.2 g

Ingredients and Quantity

- 2 zucchinis
- 4 tomatoes
- 1 tbsp. herbs
- 1 garlic clove
- Black pepper and salt, to taste

Direction

1. Diced zucchini and put into a pan.
2. Add peeled, seedless tomatoes as well as herbs.
3. Cook in the air fryer on low heat for 35 to 40 minutes.
4. At the end of cooking, add the squeezed garlic.
5. Season adequately using salt along with pepper. Serve and enjoy!

Squash Millets in Tomato Sauce

Servings: 4

Total Time: 1 Hour 15 Minutes

Calories: 165

Fat: 3 g

Protein: 11 g

Carbs: 4 g

Fiber: 1.6 g

Ingredients and Quantity

- 6 large squashes
- 500 g chopped tomatoes
- 1 onion, large
- 1 garlic clove

- 1 basil sauce
- Salt, to taste
- 1 tbsp. sunflower oil

Direction

1. In a 300ml water pan, add the onion, the clove of garlic, chopped basil and tomatoes and sunflower oil.
2. Using a slicer, cut the squash in length.
3. Overlay one layer of squash and one layer of tomato sauce and so on until a baking sheet is completed.
4. Preheat air fryer to 180 degrees for 10 minutes.
5. Then cook for 35 minutes. Serve and enjoy!

Mexican Style Hamburger

Servings: 1

Total Time: 28 Minutes

Calories: 321

Fat: 27 g

Protein: 20 g

Carbs: 2 g

Fiber: 3.2 g

Ingredients and Quantity

- 250 g ground beef
- 4 pinches Mexican seasoning mix
- 2 medium tomatoes

Direction

1. Make hamburgers by mixing ground beef with seasonings.
2. Fry in a lightly oiled air fryer over high heat in an air fryer to grill without overcooking.
3. In another air fryer, simmer, cook peeled, and diced tomatoes with seasoning mixture until creamy.
4. Cover the hamburgers with the sauce and serve immediately. Enjoy!

Hungarian Style Hamburger

Servings: 4

Total Time: 24 Minutes

Calories: 280

Fat: 22 g

Protein: 13 g

Carbs: 2 g

Fiber: 2.8 g

Ingredients and Quantity

- 6 small onions
- 1 red bell pepper
- 500 g 5% fat ground beef
- 2 tbsp. paprika
- 100 ml tomato sauce
- 1 pinch cayenne
- 1/2 lemon
- 80 g curd with 0% fat
- Black pepper and salt, to taste

Direction

1. Peel and chop the onions, wash the peppers, remove the seeds and dice.
2. Lightly grease an air fryer and sauté onion and pepper for 5 minutes over low heat in an air fryer.
3. Remove the vegetables from the pan and fry the meat for 2 minutes over high heat, kneading with a fork.
4. Add paprika, tomato sauce, onion, and bell pepper.
5. Cook for another 2 minutes, mixing and seasoning with Black pepper and salt and cayenne.
6. Squeeze the lemon juice, add to the curd and beat.
7. Out of the heat, add the sauce to the mixture and heat without boiling.
8. Serve immediately. Enjoy!

Stroganoff Beef Kebab

Servings: 2

Total Time: 30 Minutes

Calories: 224

Fat: 13 g

Protein: 18 g

Carbs: 10 g

Fiber: 2.2 g

Ingredients and Quantity

- 500 g tomatoes
- 1 garlic clove, grated
- 600 g lean beef
- 200 g pepper
- 200 g onion
- Lemon juice
- Herbs of your choice

- Black pepper and salt, to taste

Direction

1. Peel tomatoes, remove seeds, and mash them.
2. In an air fryer, sauté the tomatoes with the garlic over low heat. Season it.
3. Cut the meat, peppers, and onions into pieces. Put them in kebabs and broil for about 10 minutes in the air fryer or on a barbecue grill.
4. When serving, remove the ingredients from the skewers, drizzle them with lemon, and season with the herbs.
5. Put some tomato sauce on each plate.
6. Set the seasoning and sprinkle the parsley. Enjoy!

Stuffed Zucchini

Servings: 4

Total Time: 40 Minutes

Calories: 170

Fat: 12 g

Protein: 20 g

Carbs: 8 g

Fiber: 1.7 g

Ingredients and Quantity

- 4 zucchinis
- 500 g lean ground beef
- A jar green parsley (Mexican product, green tomato sauce with pepper)
- 200 g 0% fat cottage cheese
- Black pepper and salt, to taste

Direction

1. Cut the zucchini in two vertically. Remove the seeds.
2. Season adequately using salt along with pepper.
3. Stir in meat, green parsley, and cottage cheese.
4. Fill the zucchinis with the mixture.
5. Cook in an air fryer for 30 minutes at 240 degrees. Serve and enjoy!

Zucchini Chicken Papers

Servings: 4

Total Time: 30 Minutes

Calories: 341

Fat: 5 g

Protein: 3 g

Carbs: 6 g

Fiber: 1.7 g

Ingredients and Quantity

- 8 chicken breasts
- 4 zucchinis
- 1 garlic clove
- 1 lemon
- 2 peeled tomatoes

Direction

1. Preheat air fryer to 210 degrees.
2. Cut chicken breasts into small slices.
3. Wash and cut the zucchinis into slices. Peel and chop the garlic. Chop the lemon.
4. In an air fryer, sauté the zucchini, tomatoes, garlic, and lemon over high heat.
5. Then remove from heat. Cut 4 pieces of parchment paper into a rectangle.
6. Distribute the chicken and vegetables in these rectangles, and close them.
7. Cook in air fryer for 15 to 20 minutes. Serve and enjoy!

Salmon with Green Parsley and Cherry Tomatoes

Servings: 2

Total Time: 60 Minutes

Calories: 248

Fat: 10 g

Protein: 35 g

Carbs: 3 g

Fiber: 2.4 g

Ingredients and Quantity

- 2 salmon fillets
- 300 g cherry tomatoes
- 2 pinches fish herbs
- 1 jar salsa Verde (Mexican sauce)

Direction

1. In a parchment paper wrap the salmon and cherry tomatoes cut in two.
2. Sprinkle the herbs and add the green parsley.
3. Cook for 45 minutes at 200 degrees in the air fryer.

4. Because green parsley is salty enough, no salt is required. Serve and enjoy!

Mexican Stylish Shrimps

Servings: 4

Total Time: 13 Minutes

Calories: 99

Fat: 3 g

Protein: 16 g

Carbs: 0 g

Fiber: 0.9 g

Ingredients and Quantity

- 4 tomatoes
- 1 green bell pepper
- 2 tbsp. chopped cilantro
- 1 lemon
- 1 garlic clove
- 32 prawns
- Salt, to taste

Direction

1. Mix peeled, seedless, diced tomatoes with peeled pepper.
2. Chop the cilantro and remove the lemon juice.
3. Add garlic and salt. Steam the prawns in the air fryer for 2 to 3 minutes.
4. Mix in the sauce. Serve and enjoy!

Air Fryer Squid

Servings: 4

Total Time: 1 Hour 15 Minutes

Calories: 251

Fat: 5 g

Protein: 17 g

Carbs: 3 g

Fiber: 2.5 g

Ingredients and Quantity

- 1 to 2 chopped onions

- 2 cans whole tomatoes
- 1 pepper
- 2 to 3 peeled and mashed garlic cloves
- 1 bundle herbs of your choice
- 1 strong pepper
- 500 squid rings
- Black pepper and salt

Direction

1. In a lightly greased air fryer oil in the air fryer (remove excess with paper towels), sauté the chopped onions at medium temperature.
2. Meanwhile, scald and peel the tomatoes.
3. When the onion is very golden, add the crushed tomatoes and herbs and spices.
4. Cook in the air fryer for 10 minutes over low heat, without lid.
5. Drain the water and wash the squids.
6. Add them to the sauce and simmer for 45 minutes. Serve and enjoy!

Fish Terrine with Chives

Servings: 3

Total Time: 1 Hour 25 Minutes

Calories: 235

Fat: 11 g

Protein: 14 g

Carbs: 3 g

Fiber: 2.5 g

Ingredients and Quantity

- 200 g carrot
- 400 g golden or cod
- 4 egg whites
- 2 tbsp. cottage cheese with 0% fat
- 300 g fresh salmon
- 300 g spinach, cooked and well drained

For the Sauce:

- 500 ml 0% fat curd, or a 0% fat yogurt
- Lemon juice
- Some chive stems or tarragon
- Black pepper and salt, to taste

Direction

Note: The recipe should be prepared the day before the tasting.

1. Steam the carrot for 10 minutes and pass in a blender.
2. Put the gold in a blender and mix with egg whites and cottage cheese.
3. Season adequately using salt along with pepper.
4. Divide the mixture into three parts.
5. In one of them, add the carrot puree.
6. In the other, spinach (cooked and beaten in a blender the day before). The last part should not be mixed.
7. In a paper-lined form, place one layer of each mixture, separated by a layer of sliced salmon.
8. Cook in the air fryer at 180 degrees for 45 minutes.

For the sauce:

9. Mix the curd, lemon juice and herbs. Serve and enjoy!

Tuna Cream

Servings: 2

Total Time: 35 Minutes

Calories: 188

Fat: 11 g

Protein: 15 g

Carbs: 7 g

Fiber: 1.8 g

Ingredients and Quantity

*   500 ml water
*   200 g canned tuna, fat-free
*   1 onion
*   1 garlic clove
*   300 g zucchini
*   3 tbsp. tomato paste
*   Black pepper and salt, to taste

Direction

1. Heat the water in a pan.
2. Crumble the tuna.
3. Peel and then chop the onion and garlic.
4. Wash, peel and slice the zucchini.
5. In salt water, add tuna, onion, garlic, zucchini and tomato paste. Add black pepper.
6. Cover and cook in the air fryer for 25 minutes. Serve and enjoy!

KETOGENIC DIET TIPS

Ketogenic diet is a diet plan that puts your body's innate intelligence to work by forcing your body to enter into a state of ketosis (a state during which your body relies on fat for energy instead of carbohydrates). Your body already instinctively knows how to do this when you don't eat carbohydrates, but the point of the ketogenic diet is to force it to happen and keep it going for as long as you want. If you're interested in starting a ketogenic diet, a qualified nutrition or healthcare professional can help you get started.

What is Ketogenic Diet?

The ketogenic diet encourages you to get most of your calories from fat and severely restrict carbohydrates. Unlike a typical low-carbohydrate diet, the ketogenic diet is not a high-protein diet. Instead, it's a high-fat, moderate-protein, and low-carbohydrate diet. Although your exact macronutrient ratio will differ based on your individual needs, a typical nutritional ketogenic diet looks something like this:

- **Fat:** 60–75 percent of calories
- **Protein:** 15–30 percent of calories
- **Carbohydrates:** 5–10 percent of calories

These are just general guidelines, but most people on a successful ketogenic diet fall somewhere in this range. In order to figure what you should be eating, you'll have to calculate your individual macronutrient ratios. As your diet progresses and your body begins to change, you may have to recalculate these numbers and make the proper adjustments to your diet plan.

Types of Keto Diets

Here are the common types of keto diets we have.

1. **Standard ketogenic diet (SKD):** This is characterized by a very low-carb, moderate-protein and high-fat diet. It typically includes 75% fat, 20% protein and only 5% carbs.
2. **Cyclical ketogenic diet (CKD):** This diet requires periods of higher-carb "refeeds"; for example, 5 ketogenic days followed by 2 high-carb days.
3. **Targeted ketogenic Diet (TKD):** This diet requires adding carbs around physical workouts.
4. **High-protein ketogenic Diet (HKD):** This has features in common with a standard ketogenic diet, but contains more protein. It contains 60% fat, 35% protein and 5% carbs.

How to Calculate Your Macronutrient Ratio

The first thing you need to do to calculate your macronutrient ratio is figure out how many calories you should be eating. There are several online calculators that can calculate this number for you, but to do it yourself, you can use a method called the Mifflin-St. Jeor formula, which looks like this:

- **Men:** $10 \times$ weight (kg) $+ 6.25 \times$ height (cm) $- 5 \times$ age (y) $+ 5$
- **Women:** $10 \times$ weight (kg) $+ 6.25 \times$ height (cm) $- 5 \times$ age (y) $- 161$

To make this explanation easier, let's try using the equation with a thirty-year-old, 160-pound (72.7 kg) woman who is 5 feet 5 inches (165.1 cm) tall. When you plug this woman's statistics into the Mifflin-St. Jeor formula, you can see that she should be eating 1,448 calories per day. Now you'll use the estimated macronutrient percentages to calculate how much of each nutrient she needs to consume in order to follow a successful ketogenic diet plan.

Foods to Eat on a Ketogenic Diet

1. All dairy and plant fats are ideal for the ketogenic diet. This includes all forms of plants, oils, butter, ghee, cream, and cheese.
2. All dairy products except milk are suitable for a ketogenic diet. Since milk contains high traces of carbohydrates, it is restricted. When milk is processed to produce yogurt, cream cheese, cream, and other cheeses, the carbs are broken down making them keto-friendly.
3. All vegetables low in carbs are allowed on the ketogenic diet including all greens, above-ground vegetables, onions, garlic, ginger, and similar vegetables.
4. While most fruits should be limited or avoided, all berries and similar fruits are keto-friendly.
5. All sugar-free chocolates, sauces, and syrups are safe to use on a ketogenic diet.
6. Ketogenic sugar substitutes are allowed.
7. Nut-based milk like almond milk, coconut milk, hemp milk, soy milk, etc. are also low- carb and, thus, safe to use.

Foods to Avoid on a Ketogenic Diet

1. All grains, legumes, lentils, and beans are rich in carbohydrates, so avoid them in any form. Rice, wheat, barley, oats, chickpeas, kidney beans, corn, sorghum, etc. are all a part of this category, too.
2. Potatoes, yams, beets, yellow squash, and similar vegetables are considered starchy vegetables, and are high in carbs and should be avoided.
3. Apples, bananas, peaches, pears, melons, watermelons, mangoes, pineapples, and similar fruits are all carb-rich and are not allowed on the ketogenic diet.
4. Any amount of animal milk is restricted. Replace that with nut-based milks.
5. Flours from grains and lentils like wheat flour, all-purpose flours, and chickpea flour should be avoided and replaced with nut-based gluten-free flours.
6. White sugars, brown sugars, sugary syrups and beverages, maple syrups, honey, and dates are all forbidden on a ketogenic diet. Replace them with ketogenic sweeteners to add sweetness.
7. All processed foods with traces of carbohydrates need to be avoided.

Recommended Gluten-Free Ketogenic Flours

Flours are an important component of all baked desserts, breads, and confectioneries so they can't be altogether avoided. Since grain- and lentil-based flours are not suitable for the ketogenic diet, look to other gluten-free options to produce the same products with a lower carb content. Those include:

1. **Almond Flour:** This flour comes from almonds finely ground into a powder and is used for baking low-carb breads and desserts. There are two varieties available for almond flour: blanched and unblanched almond flour. The former is from blanched and peeled almonds whereas the latter is obtained from grinding the raw nuts. Blanched flour is more refined and mostly used for making bread and other desserts. Unblanched flour is less refined and not purely off-white in color. Instead, it has mixed shades of white and brown. Blanched flour is completely off-white in color with a fluffier texture.

2. **Almond Meal:** Almond meal is not the same as almond flour. Meal is coarser and not ideal for every bread, dessert or confectionery. Instead, it's only used when you need a crumbly texture for a recipe. Keep this differentiation in your mind when choosing ingredients; don't substitute one for the other.

3. **Coconut Flour:** Coconut flour, as the name indicates, comes from the dehydrated white flesh of a coconut. It is so finely ground that it turns into flour and gives a nice texture and taste to recipes. When it comes to texture, coconut flour is not exactly like wheat flour; it is denser and can soak up more moisture than wheat flour. Due to this, extra water or liquid needs to be added to give coconut flour the same texture batters or doughs. This flour can also make lots of clumps in a batter; use a good beater or whisk your mixtures well with a fork to break up any clumps.

4. **Ground Flaxseed:** Flaxseeds are a rich source of healthy fats, vitamins, minerals, and antioxidants making them quite beneficial for digestion and heart health. Flaxseed flour and meal can both be used in the ketogenic diet. Flaxseed bread, muffins, and cookie recipes are in this book to give you a simple idea on how to use this super nourishing seed flour or meal. Like almond meal, flaxseed meal is coarser than the ground flour so take that into account when following recipes. Processed flaxseed flour is available at most grocery stores.

5. **Psyllium Husk Powder:** This commonly known husk is obtained from the seeds of Plantago ovata. Basically, it is a good soluble fiber supplement. Available in both powder and husk form, this supplement is also good for the ketogenic diet. The powder is suitable to use in several ketogenic breads, desserts, and confectioneries as it has a light and airy touch that gives food a fluffy and soft texture.

Recommended Low Carb Sweeteners for Baking

Sweeteners play an important part in building the right balance of flavor in baked desserts. It's not just cakes or cookies that need sweeteners. Almost all desserts from custard to mousses, fat bombs, and ice creams need a good sweetener. Since sugar is not an option on a ketogenic diet, you should rely on other low-carb substitutes that are specially manufactured for such a diet. Those substitutes mainly include:

1. **Stevia:** Stevia is the strongest of all and tastes 200 times sweeter than ordinary white sugar. It should be used in very small amounts. It is available in a range of varieties including powdered and liquid form. Be extra careful while adding this intense sweetener to your recipes. One cup of sugar can be replaced with a teaspoon of stevia powder to get the same sweetness. Stevia is completely natural and comes from the stevia plant so it doesn't have any negative effects on your health.

2. **Erythritol:** Erythritol is a sugar alcohol. These kinds of substances do taste sweet, but don't contain many calories and carbohydrates. Since erythritol has a sweetness level close to that of ordinary sugar, it is more commonly used for ketogenic desserts. As you'll see on the chart, its conversion is simpler than stevia, too. Another plus point for erythritol is that it contains an extremely low amount of calories. Where one gram of sugar has around four calories, the same amount of erythritol contains only 0.24 calories. Erythritol is available in a powdered form and can be used easily in baking.

3. **Xylitol:** Xylitol is also a naturally occurring sugar alcohol that can be used to sweeten ketogenic desserts. Where other sweeteners discussed above are used for cakes and cookies, xylitol is best suited for ketogenic candies and gums. This is probably due to the taste and texture of this natural sweetener. It comes from plants like fruits and vegetables. Due to its health benefits and curing powers, it is also added to medicines and mints to keep the gums and breath fresh. It is not only low in carbohydrates, but it contains few calories and ranks very low on the glycemic index.

4. **Sorbitol:** Another sugar alcohol, sorbitol is found in several fruits and it is also present in corn syrup. It is also known as a nutritive sweetener since it can provide as many as 2.6 kcals per gram. Like xylitol, it is also great for sweets, candies, mints, gummies, and bites. It has other medicinal properties that make it

good for older people. Whether it's keto or any other diet, the use of this sweetener is always good for your health. It is 60 percent the sweetness of sugar so 1 cup of sugar can be replace with 1 ¼ cups of sorbitol.

5. **Other Recommended Sweeteners:** Swerve is another ketogenic sweetener not only used in baking, but also for ice creams, mousses, fat bombs, and other desserts. Since Swerve is available in all forms including powder, granulated, white, and even brown making it perfect for adding texture to different baked items.

    Monk fruit sweetener is another good option to sweeten your ketogenic desserts and to give them nice taste and texture.

Understanding Ketosis

The Human body is very intelligent, with many sensitive systems. It knows exactly what it wants, and knows exactly what it needs to do to get what it wants. What your body wants is energy. Without energy, your cells starve and you die. Your body has several metabolic pathways it can use to convert the food you eat into energy. The default metabolic pathway uses glucose from carbohydrates consumed as fuel. As long as you provide your body with carbohydrates, it uses them as energy while storing the excess as fat in the process. When you deny your body carbohydrates, it needs to get the energy somewhere else to survive.

What Is Ketosis?

Your body's second preferred source of energy is fat. When carbohydrates are not easily accessible, your body turns to fat to get vital energy. The liver will break down fat into fatty acids, which then break down into an energy-rich substance called ketones. When your body burns fats instead of carbohydrates for energy, the process is called ketosis. The goal of a ketogenic diet is to kick your body into long-term ketosis, ultimately turning it into a fat-burning machine.

LOW CARB KETO AIR FRYER RECIPES

Strictly for those living a ketogenic lifestyle who wish to reach their keto targets faster.

Breakfast Recipes

Chicken Strips

Servings: 4

Total Time: 20 Minutes

Calories: 245

Fat: 11.5 g

Protein: 33 g

Carbs: 0.6 g

Fiber: 2.4 g

Ingredients and Quantity

- 1 lb. chicken fillets
- 1 tsp. paprika
- 1 tbsp. cream
- 1/2 tsp. salt and pepper

Direction

1. Dice the fillets into strips. Season to your liking with the salt and pepper.
2. Set the Air Fryer at 365°F and add the butter to the basket.
3. Arrange the strips in the basket and air fry for 6 minutes.
4. Flip the strips and cook for another 5 minutes.
5. When done, sprinkle with the cream and paprika.
6. Serve warm. Enjoy!

Egg Pizza

Servings: 1

Total Time: 15 Minutes

Calories: 285

Fat: 18 g

Protein: 22 g

Carbs: 8 g

Fiber: 2.8 g

Ingredients and Quantity

- 2 eggs
- 1/2 tsp. dried oregano
- 1/2 tsp. dried basil
- 2 tbsp. shredded mozzarella cheese
- 4 thin slices pepperoni
- 1 ramekin

Direction

1. Whisk the eggs with the oregano and basil.
2. Pour into the ramekin and top off with the pepperoni and cheese.
3. Arrange the ramekin in the air fryer.
4. Cook for 3 minutes and serve. Enjoy!

Eggs in a Zucchini Nest

Servings: 4

Total Time: 20 Minutes

Calories: 221

Fat: 17.7 g

Protein: 13.4 g

Carbs: 2.9 g

Fiber: 2.2 g

Ingredients and Quantity

- 8 oz. grated zucchini
- 4 tsp. butter
- 1/4 tsp. sea salt
- 1/2 tsp. black pepper
- 1/2 tsp. paprika
- 4 eggs
- 4 oz. shredded cheddar cheese
- 4 ramekins

Direction

1. Preheat the Air Fryer at 356°F.
2. Grate the zucchini.

3. Add the butter to the ramekins and add the zucchini in a nest shape. Sprinkle with the paprika, salt, and pepper.
4. Whisk the eggs and add to the nest, topping it off with the cheese.
5. Air fry for 7 minutes.
6. Chill for 3 minutes and serve in the ramekin. Enjoy!

Bacon and Cheese Muffins

Servings: 6

Total Time: 60 Minutes

Calories: 251

Fat: 20 g

Protein: 12 g

Carbs: 6 g

Fiber: 2.5 g

Ingredients and Quantity

- 1 large egg
- 4 large slices bacon
- 1 medium diced onion
- 2 tbsp. olive oil
- 2 tsp. baking powder
- 1 cup milk
- 1 cup shredded cheddar cheese
- 1 1/2 cup almond flour
- 1 tsp. parsley
- Salt and pepper, to taste
- 6 muffin tins to fit in the basket

Direction

1. Set the temperature on the Air Fryer to 356°F.
2. Prepare the bacon slices with a small amount of oil. Add the onion when it's about ¾ ready.
3. Sauté and set aside when translucent. Drain on towels.
4. Mix the rest of the fixings and stir well. Add the onions and bacon.
5. Stir well and add the batter into 6 muffin holders. Add to the fryer basket for 20 minutes.
6. Lower the heat for 10 minutes (320°F). Serve and enjoy hot!

Mushroom, Onion and Cheese Frittata

Servings: 2

Total Time: 30 Minutes

Calories: 284

Fat: 22 g

Protein: 17 g

Carbs: 6 g

Fiber: 2.8 g

Ingredients and Quantity

- 1 tbsp. olive oil
- 2 cups sliced mushrooms
- 1 small sliced onion
- 3 eggs
- 1/2 cup grated cheese
- Salt, to taste
- 1 skillet

Direction

1. Program the Air Fryer to 320°F.
2. Warm up a skillet (medium heat) and add the oil.
3. Toss in the mushrooms and onions and sauté for about 5 minutes. Add to the Air Fryer.
4. Whisk the eggs with the salt and dump on top of the fixings in the fryer.
5. Sprinkle with the cheese and air fry for 10 minutes.
6. Take right out of the basket and serve. Enjoy!

Eggs, Ham and Spinach

Servings: 4

Total Time: 40 Minutes

Calories: 190

Fat: 13 g

Protein: 15 g

Carbs: 3 g

Fiber: 1.9 g

Ingredients and Quantity

- 7 oz. sliced ham
- 2 1/4 cup spinach
- 4 tsp. cream milk
- 1 tbsp. olive oil
- 4 large eggs
- Salt and pepper, to taste

- 4 ramekins
- Cooking spray
- 1 skillet

Direction

1. Set the fryer temperature to 356°F.
2. Spray the ramekins.
3. Warm up the oil in a skillet (medium heat) and sauté the spinach until wilted. Drain.
4. Divide the spinach and rest of the fixings in each of the ramekins.
5. Sprinkle with the salt and pepper.
6. Bake until set (20 minutes).
7. Serve when they are to your liking. Enjoy!

Breakfast Soufflé

Servings: 4

Total Time: 20 Minutes

Calories: 195

Fat: 15 g

Protein: 9 g

Carbs: 6 g

Fiber: 1.8 g

Ingredients and Quantity

- 6 eggs
- 1/3 cup milk
- 1/2 cup mozzarella cheese, shredded
- 1 tbsp. chopped parsley
- 1/2 cup ham, chopped
- 1 tsp. salt
- 1 tsp. black pepper
- 1/2 tsp. garlic powder

Direction

1. Grease 4 ramekins with a nonstick cooking spray.
2. Preheat your air fryer to 350 degrees Fahrenheit.
3. Using a large bowl, add and stir all the ingredients until it mixes properly.
4. Pour the egg mixture into the greased ramekins and place it inside your air fryer.
5. Cook it inside your air fryer for 8 minutes.
6. Then carefully remove the soufflé from your air fryer and allow it to cool off. Serve and enjoy!

Italian Frittata

Servings: 4

Total Time: 25 Minutes

Calories: 225

Fat: 14 g

Protein: 20 g

Carbs: 4.5 g

Fiber: 2.2 g

Ingredients and Quantity

- 6 eggs
- 1/3 cup milk
- 4 oz. Italian sausage, chopped
- 3 cups chopped kale
- 1 red bell pepper, deseeded and chopped
- 1/2 cup grated feta cheese
- 1 zucchini, chopped
- 1 tbsp. basil, chopped
- 1 tsp. garlic powder
- 1 tsp. onion powder
- 1 tsp. salt, or to taste
- 1 tsp. black pepper, or to taste

Direction

1. Preheat your air fryer to 360 degrees Fahrenheit.
2. Grease the air fryer pan with a nonstick cooking spray.
3. To the pan, add Italian sausage and cook it inside your air fryer for 5 minutes.
4. While doing that, add and stir in the remaining ingredients until it mixes properly.
5. Combine the egg mixture to the pan and allow it to cook inside your air fryer for 5 minutes.
6. Thereafter carefully remove the pan and allow it to cool off until it gets chilly enough to serve. Serve and enjoy!

Air Bread and Egg Butter

Servings: 19

Total Time: 45 Minutes

Calories: 40

Fat: 3.9 g

Protein: 1.2 g

Carbs: 0.5 g

Fiber: 0.4 g

Ingredients and Quantity

- 3 eggs
- 1 tsp. baking powder
- 1/4 tsp. sea salt
- 1 cup almond flour
- 1/4 cup butter

Direction

1. Soften the butter to room temperature.
2. Whisk the eggs with a hand mixer.
3. Combine the two and add the rest of the fixings to make a dough.
4. Knead the dough and cover with a tea towel for about 10 minutes.
5. Set the Air Fryer at 350°F.
6. Air fry the bread for 15 minutes.
7. Remove the bread and let it cool down on a wooden board.
8. Slice and serve with your favorite meal or as it is. Enjoy!

Egg Butter

Servings: 4

Total Time: 30 Minutes

Calories: 164

Fat: 8.5 g

Protein: 1.2 g

Carbs: 2.7 g

Fiber: 1.6 g

Ingredients and Quantity

- 4 eggs
- 1 tsp. salt
- 4 tbsp. butter

Direction

1. Add a layer of foil to the Air Fryer basket and add the eggs. Cook at 320°F for 17 minutes. Transfer to an ice-cold water bath to chill.
2. Peel and chop the eggs and combine with the rest of the fixings. Combine well until it achieves a creamy texture.
3. Enjoy with your Air Fried Bread.

Avocado Egg Boats

Servings: 2

Total Time: 10 Minutes

Calories: 288

Fat: 26 g

Protein: 7.6 g

Carbs: 9.4 g

Fiber: 2.8 g

Ingredients and Quantity

- 1 big avocado
- 2 eggs
- Chopped chives
- Chopped parsley
- Salt and pepper, to taste

Direction

1. Warm up the fryer to 350°F.
2. Remove the pit from the avocado.
3. Slice and scoop out part of the flesh. Shake with the seasonings.
4. Add an egg to each half and place in the preheated Air Fryer for 6 minutes.
5. Remove and serve with some additional parsley and chives if desired. Enjoy!

Avocado Muffins

Servings: 7

Total Time: 30 Minutes

Calories: 133

Fat: 12.4 g

Protein: 2.2 g

Carbs: 2.9 g

Fiber: 1.3 g

Ingredients and Quantity

- 1 cup almond flour
- 1/2 tsp. baking soda
- 1 tsp. apple cider vinegar
- 1 egg
- 4 tbsp. butter

- 3 scoops stevia powder
- 1/2 cup pitted avocado
- 1 oz. melted dark chocolate

Direction

1. Preheat the Air Fryer to 355°F.
2. Whisk the almond flour, baking soda, and vinegar. Add the stevia powder and melted chocolate.
3. Whisk the egg in another container and add to the mixture along with the butter.
4. Peel, cube, and mash the avocado and add. Blend with a hand mixer to make the flour mixture smooth.
5. Pour into the muffin forms (½ full).
6. Cook for 9 minutes. Lower the heat (340°F) and cook for 3 more minutes.
7. Chill before serving for the best results. Enjoy!

Chicken Hash

Servings: 3

Total Time: 15 Minutes

Calories: 261

Fat: 16.2 g

Protein: 21 g

Carbs: 7.1 g

Fiber: 2.6 g

Ingredients and Quantity

- 7 oz. chicken fillet
- 6 oz. chopped cauliflower
- 1/2 yellow diced onion
- 1 chopped green pepper
- 1 tbsp. water
- 1 tbsp. cream
- 1 tsp. black pepper
- 3 tbsp. butter

Direction

1. Program the Air Fryer to 380°F.
2. Chop the cauliflower and add to a blender to make rice.
3. Chop the chicken into bite-sized pieces and sprinkle with salt and pepper.
4. Prepare the veggies and combine the fixings.
5. Add the fryer basket and cook until done (6-7 minutes).
6. Watch closely to prevent scorching. Serve and enjoy!

Beef Recipes

Cheesy Beef Empanadas

Servings: 6

Total Time: 50 Minutes

Calories: 283

Fat: 26.8 g

Protein: 8.7 g

Carbs: 3.6 g

Fiber: 2.8 g

Ingredients and Quantity

- 2 cups mozzarella cheese
- 1 cup cream cheese
- 1 1/2 cup almond flour
- 2 eggs
- 2 1/2 cup ground beef
- 1/4 cup butter
- 1/2 cup chopped onion
- 1/4 tsp. salt
- 1/2 tsp. black pepper
- 1/2 tsp. nutmeg

Direction

1. Place butter in a microwave-safe bowl then melts the butter.
2. Pour the melted butter over the beef then add chopped onion to the bowl.
3. Season with salt, black pepper, and nutmeg then stir well.
4. Preheat an Air Fryer to 400°F (204°C).
5. Transfer the seasoned beef to the Air Fryer then cook for 10 minutes.
6. Remove the beef from the Air Fryer then let it cool.
7. Next, place grated Mozzarella cheese and cream cheese in a microwave-safe bowl then melt the mixture.
8. Once the cheese is melted, add eggs to the bowl then stir until incorporated.
9. Stir in almond flour to the cheese mixture then mix until becoming a soft dough.
10. Place the dough on a flat surface then roll until thin.
11. Using a circle cookies mold cut the thin dough into 12.
12. Put about 2 tbsp. of beef on a circle dough then fold until becoming a half-circle. Glue with water.
13. Repeat with the remaining dough and beef then set aside.
14. Preheat an Air Fryer to 425°F (218°C).
15. Arrange the beef empanadas in the Air Fryer then cook for 12 minutes or until lightly golden brown.
16. Remove from the Air Fryer then serve warm. Enjoy!

Cheesy Melt Beef Bombs

Servings: 4

Total Time: 50 Minutes

Calories: 436

Fat: 36.2 g

Protein: 22.5 g

Carbs: 4.3 g

Fiber: 4.3 g

Ingredients and Quantity

- 1 lb. ground beef
- 1 cup chopped onion
- 1/4 tsp. salt
- 1/2 tsp. pepper
- 3 egg yolks
- 1 cup grated mozzarella cheese
- 1 tbsp. extra virgin olive oil

Direction

1. Put the ground beef, and chopped onion in a bowl then season with salt and pepper.
2. Add egg yolks to the beef mixture then mix until combined.
3. Shape the ground beef mixture into small or medium balls and fill each beef ball with grated Mozzarella cheese.
4. Preheat an Air Fryer to 375°F (191°C).
5. Place the beef balls in the Air Fryer then spray with olive oil.
6. Set the time to 10 minutes and cook the beef balls.
7. Once it is done, remove the beef balls from the Air Fryer then serve. Enjoy!

Jalapeno Spicy Fried Beef

Servings: 8

Total Time: 60 Minutes

Calories: 444

Fat: 35.3 g

Protein: 25.4 g

Carbs: 7 g

Fiber: 4.4 g

Ingredients and Quantity

113

- 1 beef roast
- 2 jalapenos
- 2 tbsp. coconut oil
- 1/4 tsp. salt
- 1/2 tsp. black pepper
- 2 tbsp. lemon juice
- 3 tbsp. minced garlic
- 1/2 cup chopped onion
- 1 cup sliced bell pepper
- 1/2 cup butter
- 1 tsp. cayenne
- 1 tbsp. red chili flakes
- 1 tbsp. hot sauce
- 1 tbsp. dried parsley

Direction

1. Cut the jalapenos into small pieces then combine with salt, black pepper, lemon juice, and minced garlic.
2. Season the beef roast with the spice mixture then let it rest for a few minutes.
3. Preheat an Air Fryer to 400°F (204°C).
4. Once the Air Fryer is ready, place the seasoned beef roast in the Air Fryer then spray with coconut oil.
5. Sprinkle chopped onion and sliced bell pepper on over the beef roast then cook for 18 minutes.
6. Meanwhile, melt butter in a saucepan then remove from heat.
7. Add cayenne, red chili flakes, hot sauce, and dried parsley then stir until combined.
8. Once the beef roast is done, drizzle the butter sauce over the beef roast then cook for another 20 minutes.
9. Transfer the cooked beef roast to a serving dish, then enjoy.

Rosemary Rib Eye Beef Steak

Servings: 2

Total Time: 1 Hour 30 Minutes

Calories: 544

Fat: 49.2 g

Protein: 20.8 g

Carbs: 6 g

Fiber: 4.4 g

Ingredients and Quantity

- 2 rib eye beef steak
- 1/4 cup chopped rosemary
- 2 tsp. minced garlic
- 1/4 cup butter

- 1 1/2 tbsp. balsamic vinegar
- 1/2 tsp. salt
- 1/2 tsp. black pepper

Direction

1. Allow the butter to melt in a saucepan over low heat then add minced garlic to the saucepan. Sauté until aromatic.
2. Remove from heat then season with balsamic vinegar, salt, and pepper. Let it cool.
3. Add chopped rosemary to the mixture then stir well.
4. Place the rib eye in a zipper-lock plastic bag then add the spice mixture to the plastic bag.
5. Shake the plastic bag and make sure the rib eye is completely seasoned.
6. Marinate the rib eye for at least an hour and store in the fridge to keep it fresh.
7. After an hour, remove the seasoned rib eye from the fridge then thaw at room temperature.
8. Preheat an Air Fryer to 400°F (204°C) and place a rack in it.
9. Once the Air Fryer is preheated, place the seasoned rib eye in the rack then cook for 15 minutes.
10. Once it is done, remove from the Air Fryer then transfer to a serving dish. Serve and enjoy!

Beef Rib Steak with Parsley Lemon Butter

Servings: 4

Total Time: 60 Minutes

Calories: 432

Fat: 42.7 g

Protein: 10.6 g

Carbs: 4.1 g

Fiber: 4.3 g

Ingredients and Quantity

- 2 beef rib eye steak
- 2 tbsp. extra virgin olive oil
- 1/4 tsp. salt
- 1/2 tsp. pepper
- 1/2 cup butter
- 1/4 cup chopped fresh parsley
- 2 garlic cloves
- 1/4 tsp. grated lemon zest
- 2 tbsp. lemon juice
- 1 tsp. basil
- 1/4 tsp. cayenne

Direction

1. Brush the beef rib eye steak with olive oil then sprinkle salt and pepper over the beef. Let it sit for about 30 minutes.
2. Meanwhile, place butter in a bowl then pours lemon juice over the butter.
3. Using a fork mix until the butter is smooth.
4. Grate the garlic then add to the butter.
5. Stir in chopped fresh parsley, grated lemon zest, basil, and cayenne to the butter then mix well. Store in the fridge.
6. Preheat an Air Fryer to 400°F (204°C) and put a rack in the Air Fryer.
7. Place the seasoned beef rib eye on the rack then set the time to 15 minutes. Cook the beef.
8. Once the beef rib eye is ready, remove from the Air Fryer then place on a serving dish.
9. Serve with the butter sauce. Enjoy!

Marinated Flank Steak with Beef Gravy

Servings: 2

Total Time: 3 Hours 40 Minutes

Calories: 432

Fat: 42.7 g

Protein: 10.6 g

Carbs: 4.1 g

Fiber: 4.3 g

Ingredients and Quantity

- 1 flank steak
- 1/4 cup butter
- 3 1/2 tbsp. lemon juice
- 1/2 tsp. salt
- 1/2 tsp. pepper
- 1 cup chopped onion
- 1/4 cup beef broth
- 2 tbsp. coconut milk
- 3 tbsp. coconut aminos
- 1 tsp. nutmeg
- 1 scoop stevia
- 1 tbsp. extra virgin olive oil

Direction

1. Allow the butter to melt in the microwave then let it cool.
2. Combine the melted butter with lemon juice, minced garlic, salt, and pepper then mix well.
3. Season the flank steak with the spice mixture then marinate for at least 3 hours. Store in the refrigerator to keep it fresh.
4. Preheat a saucepan over medium heat then pour olive oil into the saucepan.
5. Once the oil is hot, stir in chopped onion then sauté until translucent and aromatic.

6. Pour beef broth into the saucepan then season with nutmeg. Bring to boil.
7. Once it is boiled, reduce the heat then add coconut milk, coconut aminos, and stevia to the saucepan. Stir until dissolved.
8. Get the sauce off heat then let it cool.
9. After 3 hours, remove the seasoned flank steak from the refrigerator then thaw at room temperature.
10. Preheat an Air Fryer to 400°F (204°C).
11. Once the Air Fryer is ready, place the seasoned flank steak in the Air Fryer then set the time to 15 minutes.
12. After 15 minutes, open the Air Fryer then drizzle the beef gravy over the flank steak.
13. Cook the flank steak again and set the time to 5 minutes.
14. Remove the cooked flank steak from the Air Fryer then place on a serving dish.
15. Drizzle the gravy on top then enjoy right away. Enjoy!

Buttery Beef Loin and Cheese Sauce

Servings: 3

Total Time: 40 Minutes

Calories: 441

Fat: 39.4 g

Protein: 15.7 g

Carbs: 5.6 g

Fiber: 4.4 g

Ingredients and Quantity

- 1 lb. beef loin
- 1 tbsp. butter
- 1 tbsp. minced garlic
- 1/2 tsp. salt
- 1/2 tsp. dried parsley
- 1/4 tsp. thyme
- 1/2 cup sour cream
- 3/4 cup cream cheese
- 2 tbsp. grated cheddar cheese
- 1/4 tsp. pepper
- 1/4 tsp. nutmeg

Direction

1. Place butter in a microwave-safe bowl then melts the butter.
2. Combine with minced garlic, salt, dried parsley, and thyme then mix well.
3. Cut the beef loin into slices then brush with the butter mixture.
4. Preheat an Air Fryer to 400°F (204°C).

5. Once the Air Fryer is ready, place the seasoned beef loin in the Air Fryer and set the time to 15 minutes. Cook the beef loin.
6. Meanwhile, place cream cheese in a mixing bowl then using an electric mixer beat until smooth and fluffy.
7. Add sour cream, and grated cheese then seasons with pepper and nutmeg. Beat again until fluffy then store in the fridge.
8. Once the beef loin is done, remove from the Air Fryer then place on a serving dish.
9. Serve and enjoy with cheese sauce.

Savory Pecan Beef Ribs

Servings: 4

Total Time: 3 Hours 40 Minutes

Calories: 396

Fat: 38 g

Protein: 12.4 g

Carbs: 5.2 g

Fiber: 3.9 g

Ingredients and Quantity

- 1/2 beef ribs
- 1 tbsp. lemon juice
- 1 egg
- 3 tbsp. coconut milk
- 1 cup roasted pecans
- 1 tsp. ginger
- 1/4 tsp. cayenne
- 1/4 tsp. salt
- 1/2 tsp. pepper
- 1 tbsp. extra virgin olive oil

Direction

1. Splash lemon juice over the beef ribs then let it rest for a few minutes.
2. Meanwhile, crack the egg then pour coconut milk into the egg. Stir until incorporated.
3. Place roasted pecans in a food processor then season with ginger, cayenne, salt, and pepper. Process until becoming flour texture.
4. Dip the beef ribs in the egg mixture then roll into the pecan mixture. Make sure the rib is completely coated with the pecans.
5. Preheat an Air Fryer to 400°F (204°C) and put a rack in the Air Fryer.
6. Once the Air Fryer is ready, place the coated beef ribs on the rack.
7. Spray olive oil over the beef ribs then cook the beef ribs. Set the time to 15 minutes.
8. Once it is done, remove from the Air Fryer and serve warm. Enjoy!

Beef Meatloaf Tomato

Servings: 8

Total Time: 30 Minutes

Calories: 242

Fat: 19.3 g

Protein: 13.7 g

Carbs: 3.1 g

Fiber: 2.4 g

Ingredients and Quantity

- 2 cup ground beef
- 1 egg
- 1/2 cup tomato puree
- 1/2 tsp. salt
- 3/4 tsp. pepper
- 1 cup cheddar cheese cubes
- 1/4 cup chopped onion
- 3 tbsp. minced garlic

Direction

1. Crash the eggs then place in a bowl.
2. Season with salt, pepper, and minced garlic then whisk until incorporated.
3. Pour the egg mixture into the ground beef then mix well.
4. Add cheese cubes, and chopped onion to the mixture then mix until combined.
5. Transfer the beef mixture to a silicon loaf pan then spread evenly.
6. Drizzle tomato puree on top then set aside.
7. Preheat an Air Fryer to 350°F (177°C).
8. Place the silicon loaf pan on the Air Fryer rack then cook the meatloaf for 20 minutes.
9. Once it is done, remove from the Air Fryer then let it cool.
10. Cut the beef meatloaf into slices then serve. Enjoy!

Minty Beef Balls with Lemon Yogurt Dip

Servings: 8

Total Time: 25 Minutes

Calories: 230

Fat: 19.3 g

Protein: 13.1 g

Carbs: 2.2 g

Fiber: 2.3 g

Ingredients and Quantity

- 1 lb. ground beef
- 1/4 tsp. salt
- 1/4 tsp. pepper
- 3/4 tsp. cumin
- 3/4 tsp. coriander
- 3/4 tsp. cayenne pepper
- 2 tsp. minced garlic
- 1 tbsp. chopped mint leaves
- 1 tbsp. chopped parsley
- 1 egg
- 1/2 cup grated coconut
- 3/4 cup Greek yogurt
- 1/4 cup sour cream
- 2 tbsp. lemon juice
- 1/2 tsp. grated lemon zest

Direction

1. Combine ground beef with cumin, coriander, cayenne pepper, minced garlic, chopped mint leaves, and chopped parsley in a dish.
2. Season using pepper and salt then combine well.
3. Shape the beef mixture into small balls then set aside.
4. Crack the eggs then stir until incorporated.
5. Place the balls in the beaten egg then roll in the grated coconut.
6. Preheat an Air Fryer to 375°F (191°C).
7. Arrange the balls in the preheated Air Fryer then cook for 7 minutes.
8. While waiting for the beef balls, place Greek yogurt, sour cream, lemon juice, and lemon zest in a mixing bowl.
9. Beat the mixture until smooth and fluffy with an electric mixer. Store in the refrigerator.
10. Once the beef balls are done remove from the Air Fryer, then place on a serving dish.
11. Drizzle lemon yogurt over the beef balls then serve. Enjoy!

Poultry Recipes

Turkey Cilantro Creamy Butter

Servings: 4

Total Time: 1 Hour 45 Minutes

Calories: 402

Fat: 36.3 g

Protein: 16.8 g

Carbs: 4.1 g

Fiber: 4 g

Ingredients and Quantity

- 1 lb. turkey breast
- 1/2 cup cilantro
- 1 tsp. minced garlic
- 3/4 tsp. cumin
- 1/4 tsp. salt
- 1/2 tsp. pepper
- 2 tbsp. extra virgin olive oil
- 1/4 cup chicken broth
- 2 tbsp. lemon juice
- 1/2 cup butter
- 1/2 tsp. garlic powder
- 1/4 cup grated parmesan cheese

Direction

1. Cut the turkey breast into slices then set aside.
2. Combine cilantro with minced garlic, cumin, salt, and pepper then pour olive oil, chicken broth, and lemon juice into the mixing bowl. Stir until incorporated.
3. Rub the turkey breast with the spice mixture then let it sit for about 30 minutes. Store in the fridge to keep it fresh.
4. Meanwhile, combine butter with garlic powder and Parmesan cheese then using an electric mixer mix until combined and fluffy. Set aside.
5. After 30 minutes of seasoning process, take the turkey out of the fridge.
6. Preheat an Air Fryer to 350°F (177°C) and place a rack in the Air Fryer.
7. Place the seasoned turkey on the rack then cook for 20 minutes.
8. Open the Air Fryer then flip the turkey.
9. Cook the turkey again for another 20 minutes.
10. Once it is done, remove the turkey from the Air Fryer then place on a serving dish.
11. Serve and enjoy with creamy butter.

Buttery Whole Chicken

Servings: 4

Total Time: 60 Minutes

Calories: 274

Fat: 27.6 g

Protein: 5.5 g

Carbs: 2.4 g

Fiber: 2.7 g

Ingredients and Quantity

- 1 whole chicken
- 1/2 cup butter
- 1 tsp. black pepper
- 3 tbsp. minced garlic

Direction

1. Place butter in mixing bowl then add minced garlic and black pepper.
2. Using a hand mixer beat the butter until combined.
3. Smear the chicken with the butter mixture and drop the remaining butter in the chicken cavity.
4. Preheat an Air Fryer to 350°F (177°C).
5. Place the chicken in the Air Fryer then cook for 30 minutes.
6. After 30 minutes, flip the chicken and cook again for another 30 minutes.
7. Once the internal temperature of the chicken has reached 165°F (74°C), remove it from the Air Fryer.
8. Allow the chicken to settle for a few minutes then serve. Enjoy warm.

Turkey Breast with Strawberry Glaze

Servings: 4

Total Time: 1 Hour 25 Minutes

Calories: 344

Fat: 28.3 g

Protein: 15.7 g

Carbs: 7.8 g

Fiber: 3.4 g

Ingredients and Quantity

- 2 lb. turkey breast
- 1 tsp. salt
- 3/4 tsp. black pepper

- 1 tbsp. olive oil
- 1 cup fresh strawberries
- 2 tbsp. chopped shallots
- 2 tbsp. lemon juice
- 1 tbsp. coconut flour
- 1/4 cup chicken broth
- 1/2 cup butter

Direction

1. Season the turkey breast with salt and black pepper.
2. Preheat an Air Fryer to 375°F (191°C).
3. Place the turkey in the Air Fryer then cook for 15 minutes.
4. While waiting for the turkey, pour chicken broth into a saucepan then add shallots and lemon juice. Bring to boil.
5. Once it is boiled, stir in coconut flour then stir until incorporated and smooth.
6. Add butter to the saucepan then cook until the butter is melted. Remove from heat then set aside.
7. After 15 minutes of cooking time, open the Air Fryer then flip the turkey.
8. Cook the turkey for another 15 minutes.
9. Meanwhile, place the fresh strawberries in a food processor. Process until smooth.
10. Drizzle the strawberry over the turkey then cook again for 7 minutes.

Chicken Fennel

Servings: 4

Total Time: 1 Hour 25 Minutes

Calories: 414

Fat: 33.7 g

Protein: 22.5 g

Carbs: 6.4 g

Fiber: 4.1 g

Ingredients and Quantity

- 1 1/2 lb. chicken thighs
- 2 tsp. fennel
- 1 cup chopped onion
- 3/4 tbsp. coconut oil
- 1 1/2 tsp. ginger
- 2 1/2 tsp. minced garlic
- 1 1/2 tsp. smoked paprika
- 1 tsp. curry
- 1/2 tsp. turmeric
- 1/2 tsp. salt

- 1/2 tsp. pepper
- 1 1/2 cup coconut milk

Direction

1. Place fennel, chopped onion, and smoked paprika in a bowl.
2. Season with salt, minced garlic, ginger, curry, pepper, and turmeric then pour coconut oil into the mixture. Mix well.
3. Marinate the chicken thighs with the spice mixture then let them sit for 30 minutes.
4. After 30 minutes, preheat an Air Fryer to 375°F (191°C).
5. Transfer the chicken together with the spices to the Air Fryer then cook for 15 minutes.
6. After that, pour coconut milk over the chicken then stir well.
7. Cook the chicken again and set the time to 10 minutes.
8. Once it is done, arrange the chicken on a serving dish then pour the gravy over the chicken. Serve and enjoy!

Garlic Chicken Balls

Servings: 4

Total Time: 30 Minutes

Calories: 525

Fat: 46.8 g

Protein: 23.7 g

Carbs: 5.7 g

Fiber: 5.2 g

Ingredients and Quantity

- 1/2 lb. boneless chicken thighs
- 1/2 cup chopped mushroom
- 1 tsp. minced garlic
- 1 tsp. pepper
- 1/2 tsp. salt
- 1 1/4 cup roasted pecans
- 1 tsp. extra virgin olive oil

Direction

1. Cut the boneless chicken into cubes then place in a food processor.
2. Add roasted pecans to the food processor then season with minced garlic, pepper, and salt. Process until smooth.
3. Cut the mushrooms into very small dices then add to the chicken mixture.
4. Using your hand mix the chicken with diced mushrooms then shape into small balls. Set aside.
5. Preheat an Air Fryer to 375°F (191°C).
6. Brush the balls with extra virgin olive oil then arrange the chicken balls in the Air Fryer.
7. Cook the chicken balls for 18 minutes then arrange on a serving dish. Serve and enjoy!

Gingery Chicken Satay

Servings: 8

Total Time: 45 Minutes

Calories: 400

Fat: 31.7 g

Protein: 22.4 g

Carbs: 6.9 g

Fiber: 4 g

Ingredients and Quantity

- 2 lb. boneless chicken
- 2 tsp. minced garlic
- 1 tsp. ginger
- 2 tsp. sliced scallions
- 1 tsp. coriander
- 2 tbsp. coconut aminos
- 1/2 cup roasted aminos
- 1/2 cup roasted cashews
- 1 1/2 cup coconut milk

Direction

1. Cut the chicken into cubes then rub with minced garlic, ginger, sliced scallions, and coriander. Let it sit for about 15 minutes.
2. Meanwhile, place roasted cashews in a blender then pour coconut milk into the blender.
3. Add coconut aminos to the blender then blend until smooth.
4. Pour the cashews, and coconut milk mixture over the chicken then squeeze until the chicken is completely seasoned.
5. Prick the chicken with skewers then set aside.
6. Preheat an Air Fryer to 375°F (191°C).
7. Arrange the chicken satay in the Air Fryer then pour the liquid over the chicken satay.
8. Cook for 18 minutes.
9. Once it is done, remove the chicken satay from the Air Fryer then arrange on a serving dish.
10. Drizzle the gravy over the chicken satay then serve. Enjoy!

Cilantro with Green Butter

Servings: 8

Total Time: 1 Hour 40 Minutes

Calories: 399

Fat: 37.1 g

Protein: 16.3 g

Carbs: 1.4 g

Fiber: 3.9 g

Ingredients and Quantity

- 8 chicken drumsticks
- 1 cup fresh cilantro
- 1 jalapeno
- 2 tbsp. minced garlic
- 2 tbsp. ginger
- 2 1/2 tbsp. extra virgin olive oil
- 1 1/2 cups butter
- 1 3/4 tsp. salt
- 1/2 tsp. coriander
- 1/2 tsp. pepper
- 1/4 cup lemon juice

Direction

1. Chop ½ cup fresh cilantro and jalapeno then place in a bowl.
2. Add minced garlic, ginger, 1 ½ tsp. salt, olive oil, and 2 tbsp. lemon juice to the bowl. Mix well.
3. Rub the chicken drumsticks with the cilantro mixture then marinate for at least an hour to overnight. Refrigerate to stay fresh.
4. After an hour, remove the seasoned drumsticks from the fridge then thaw at room temperature.
5. Preheat an Air Fryer to 400°F (204°C).
6. Place the chicken drumsticks in the Air Fryer then cook for 18 minutes.
7. Meanwhile, place butter and the remaining fresh cilantro in a bowl.
8. Season with the remaining salt, coriander, and pepper then pour lemon juice into the bowl.
9. Using an immersion blender blend the mixture until smooth and incorporated and smooth. Set aside.
10. Once the chicken drumsticks are done, remove from the Air Fryer then place on a serving dish.
11. Serve with the green cilantro butter then enjoy immediately.

Chicken Steak Tomato

Servings: 8

Total Time: 30 Minutes

Calories: 361

Fat: 33 g

Protein: 18.1 g

Carbs: 2 g

Fiber: 3.6 g

Ingredients and Quantity

- 1 lb. boneless chicken breast
- 1/2 tsp. salt
- 1/2 tsp. pepper
- 1 cup butter
- 1 cup diced tomatoes
- 1/2 tsp. nutmeg
- 1 bay leaf
- 1 1/2 tsp. paprika
- 1/2 tsp. cloves
- 1/2 tsp. cayenne

Direction

1. Preheat an Air Fryer to 375°F (191°C).
2. Cut the chicken breast into thick slices then arrange in the Air Fryer.
3. Sprinkle salt and pepper over the chicken then cook for 15 minutes.
4. Meanwhile, melt butter over low heat then add diced tomatoes to the melted butter.
5. Season with nutmeg, bay leaf, paprika, cloves, and cayenne then bring to a simmer.
6. Once it is done, remove the sauce from heat then let it cool.
7. When the chicken is done, remove from the Air Fryer then place on a serving dish.
8. Top with tomato sauce then serves right away. Enjoy!

Chicken Curry Samosa

Servings: 4

Total Time: 30 Minutes

Calories: 365

Fat: 30.3 g

Protein: 23.1 g

Carbs: 2.5 g

Fiber: 3.6 g

Ingredients and Quantity

- 1 lb. ground chicken
- 5 tbsp. extra virgin olive oil
- 1/4 cup chopped onion
- 1/2 tsp. curry powder
- 1/4 tsp. turmeric
- 1/4 tsp. coriander
- 2 tsp. red chili flakes
- 2 tbsp. diced tomatoes
- 3/4 cup almond flour

- 1/4 cup water

Direction

1. Place ground chicken, chopped onion, curry powder, turmeric, coriander, red chili flakes, and diced tomatoes in a bowl. Mix well.
2. Preheat an Air Fryer to 375°F (191°C) and spray a tbsp. of extra virgin olive in the Air Fryer.
3. Transfer the ground chicken mixture to the Air Fryer then cook for 10 minutes.
4. Once the chicken is cooked through, transfer from the Air Fryer to a container. Let it cool.
5. Meanwhile, combine almond flour with 3 tbsp. of olive oil and water then mix until becoming dough.
6. Place the dough on a flat surface then roll until thin.
7. Using a 3-inches circle mold cookies cut the thin dough.
8. Put 2 tbsp. of chicken on circle dough then fold it.
9. Repeat with the remaining dough and chicken.
10. Preheat an Air Fryer to 400°F (204°C).
11. Brush each chicken samosa with the remaining virgin olive oil then arrange in the Air Fryer.
12. Cook the chicken samosas for 10 minutes then remove from the Air Fryer.
13. Arrange on a serving dish then serve with homemade tomato sauce or green cayenne. Enjoy warm!

Crispy Fried Chicken

Servings: 8

Total Time: 60 Minutes

Calories: 455

Fat: 41.7 g

Protein: 18 g

Carbs: 6.3 g

Fiber: 4.5 g

Ingredients and Quantity

- 1 lb. chicken thighs
- 1 tsp. salt
- 1 tsp. pepper
- 1 cup almond flour
- 1 cup water
- 2 cup roasted pecans
- 1 tsp. black pepper

Direction

1. Apply pepper and salt to the chicken thighs for seasoning and let sit for 5 minutes.
2. Meanwhile, place roasted pecans in a food processor then process until smooth and becoming flour.
3. Roll the seasoned chicken thighs in the almond flour then dip in the water.
4. Combine the remaining almond flour with pecans flour then mix well.
5. Remove the chicken thighs from water then roll in the pecans mixture.

6. Using your finger squeeze the chicken thighs until all sides of the chicken thighs are completely coated with pecans mixture.
7. Preheat an Air Fryer to 400°F (204°C).
8. Arrange the coated chicken thighs in the Air Fryer then set the time to 22 minutes.
9. Once it is done, check the doneness of the chicken thighs.
10. Give the chicken thighs an additional 5 minutes in the Air Fryer for a more golden brown color.
11. Place the crispy fried chicken on a serving dish then sprinkle black pepper on top.
12. Serve and enjoy hot.

Oregano Chicken Rolls

Servings: 8

Total Time: 60 Minutes

Calories: 393

Fat: 35 g

Protein: 15.9 g

Carbs: 7.5 g

Fiber: 3.9 g

Ingredients and Quantity

- 1/2 lb. boneless chicken breast
- 1 tsp. oregano
- 2 1/2 tsp. paprika
- 1 1/2 tsp. minced garlic
- 3/4 tsp. cumin
- 1/2 tsp. salt
- 1/2 tsp. pepper
- 1 tsp. extra virgin olive oil
- 1 bell pepper
- 1 onion
- 1 cup grated cheddar cheese
- 1/4 cup butter
- 1/4 cup Greek yogurt
- 1 egg yolk
- 2 cups roasted pecans

Direction

1. Cut the chicken breast into large-thin slices.
2. Rub the chicken with oregano, paprika, minced garlic, cumin, salt, and pepper. Set aside.
3. Cut the bell pepper into sticks then set aside.
4. Peel and chop the onion then also set aside.

5. Place a chicken slice on a flat surface then arrange bell pepper stick, chopped onion, and grated cheddar cheese on it.
6. Roll the chicken then prick with a toothpick.
7. Repeat with the remaining chicken and filling.
8. Place butter in a microwave-safe bowl then melts the butter.
9. Take the melted butter out of the microwave then add egg yolk and Greek yogurt to the melted butter.
10. Stir until incorporated then set aside.
11. Next, place roasted pecans in a food processor then process until smooth and becoming flour form.
12. Take a chicken roll then dip in the butter mixture. Roll the chicken in the pecans flour then set aside.
13. Repeat with remaining chicken rolls.
14. Preheat an Air Fryer to 375°F (191°C).
15. Arrange the chicken roll in the Air Fryer then spray with olive oil.
16. Cook the chicken roll for 14 minutes then transfer to a serving dish. Serve and enjoy!
11.
12. Remove the turkey from heat then serve with the sauce. Enjoy!

Seafood Recipes

Crispy Shrimps Coconuts

Servings: 6

Total Time: 30 Minutes

Calories: 342

Fat: 27.1 g

Protein: 19.5 g

Carbs: 6 g

Fiber: 3.4 g

Ingredients and Quantity

- 1 lb. fresh shrimps
- 1 tsp. salt
- 1 tsp. pepper
- 1 cup coconut flour
- 2 eggs
- 2 cup grated coconuts
- 2 tsp. minced garlic
- 2 tbsp. butter
- 1/2 cup cilantro
- 1 cup coconut milk
- 2 tbsp. lemon juice

Direction

1. Peel the fresh shrimps, then discard the head.
2. Rub the peeled shrimps with salt and pepper then let it sit for 5 minutes.
3. Prepare coconut flour, beaten eggs, and grated coconuts in three different bowls in a row.
4. Roll the fresh shrimps in the coconut flour then dip in beaten eggs.
5. Take the shrimps out of the beaten eggs then roll in the grated coconuts.
6. Using your finger squeeze the shrimps until all sides of the shrimps are completely coated with grated coconuts.
7. Preheat an Air Fryer to 400°F (204°C).
8. Arrange the shrimps in the Air Fryer then set the time to 10 minutes.
9. Once it is done, check the color of the shrimps.
10. Cook the shrimps for 2 minutes more for a more golden brown color.
11. Place the crispy fried shrimps in a serving dish then serve. Enjoy right away or serve with tomato sauce.

Hot Mackerel Chili

Servings: 2

Total Time: 35 Minutes

Calories: 413

Fat: 37.1 g

Protein: 21 g

Carbs: 0.7 g

Fiber: 4.1 g

Ingredients and Quantity

- 2 medium mackerels
- 1 tbsp. extra virgin olive oil
- 1 tsp. lemon juice
- 2 tsp. minced garlic
- 2 tbsp. red chili flakes
- 1/4 tsp. salt
- 1 tbsp. butter

Direction

1. Splash lemon juice over the mackerels then let it rest for about 5 minutes.
2. Rub the mackerels with minced garlic, red chili flakes, and salt then set aside.
3. Preheat an Air Fryer to 350°F (177°C).
4. Once the Air Fryer is ready, place the seasoned mackerels in the Air Fryer then cook for 5 minutes.
5. After 5 minutes, open the drawer and flip the mackerels. Cook again for another 5 minutes.
6. Remove the cooked mackerels from the Air Fryer then place on a rack.
7. Quickly brush the cooked mackerels with butter then serve. Enjoy!

Scallops with Lemon Parsley Butter

Servings: 4

Total Time: 1 Hour 20 Minutes

Calories: 307

Fat: 28.8 g

Protein: 11.1 g

Carbs: 2 g

Fiber: 3 g

Ingredients and Quantity

- 1 lb. scallops

- 1 tbsp. lemon juice
- 1/4 tsp. salt
- 1/4 tsp. pepper
- 1 1/2 tbsp. extra virgin olive oil
- 1/4 cup chopped parsley
- 1/2 cup butter
- 1/2 tsp. grated lemon zest

Direction

1. Wash scallops then pat them dry.
2. Splash lemon juice over the scallops then seasons with salt and pepper.
3. Marinate the scallops for an hour and store in the refrigerator to keep them fresh.
4. After an hour, remove the scallops from the refrigerator then thaw at room temperature.
5. Transfer the scallops to an aluminum pan.
6. Preheat an Air Fryer to 400°F (204°C) and place a rack in it.
7. Place the aluminum pan with scallops on the rack then cook for 5 minutes.
8. Remove the scallops from the Air Fryer then transfer to a serving dish.
9. Melt butter in a saucepan then removes from heat.
10. Add chopped parsley, and grated lemon zest then stir until thickened.
11. Drizzle the butter over the scallops, then serve. Enjoy right away.

Nutty Shrimps with Chili Sauce

Servings: 4

Total Time: 30 Minutes

Calories: 288

Fat: 23.9 g

Protein: 16 g

Carbs: 6.4 g

Fiber: 2.8 g

Ingredients and Quantity

- 1 lb. fresh shrimps
- 1 egg white
- 1/2 cup almond flour
- 1 cup roasted pecans
- 1 tsp. paprika
- 1/4 tsp. salt
- 1 tsp. pepper
- 1/2 cup Greek yogurt
- 2 tbsp. chili sauce

Direction

1. Peel the fresh shrimps, then discard the head. Set aside.
2. Season the egg white with salt and paprika then whisk to combine.
3. Place roasted pecans in a food processor then season with pepper. Process until smooth and becoming flour.
4. Roll the shrimps in the almond flour then dip in the seasoned egg white.
5. Next, roll the shrimps again in the pecans mixture then set aside.
6. Repeat with the remaining shrimps and flour.
7. Preheat an Air Fryer to 400°F (204°C).
8. Arrange the coated shrimps in the Air Fryer then spray with cooking spray.
9. Cook the shrimps for 5 minutes then arrange on a serving dish.
10. Combine Greek yogurt with chili sauce then mix until incorporated.
11. Drizzle the chili yogurt mixture over the shrimps then serves. Enjoy right away.

Soft Lemon Crab Cakes

Servings: 8

Total Time: 25 Minutes

Calories: 246

Fat: 20.3 g

Protein: 10.1 g

Carbs: 4.2 g

Fiber: 2.4 g

Ingredients and Quantity

- 1 lb. crabmeat
- 2 1/2 tbsp. lemon juice
- 1/2 cup diced bell pepper
- 1/4 cup chopped onion
- 1 cup mayonnaise
- 1 tbsp. yellow mustard
- 1 1/2 tsp. black pepper
- 1 1/2 tbsp. chopped parsley
- 1 1/4 tsp. garlic powder
- 1/4 tsp. cayenne pepper
- 2 tbsp. extra virgin olive oil
- 1/2 cup roasted walnuts

Direction

1. Put your walnuts which are roasted in a blender then process until smooth.
2. Add crabmeat to the food processor then season with lemon juice, yellow mustard, black pepper, garlic powder, and cayenne pepper. Process until smooth.

3. Transfer the crab and walnuts mixture to a bowl then add chopped onion and diced bell pepper to the mixture.
4. Pour mayonnaise over the mixture then mix well.
5. Split the mixture into 16 then roll into balls.
6. Press each ball using your hands until becoming patty form.
7. Repeat with the remaining patties.
8. Preheat an Air Fryer to 375°F (191°C).
9. Arrange the patties in the Air Fryer then spray with extra virgin olive oil.
10. Cook the patties for 10 minutes. You may cook them in two batches.
11. Once it is done, remove the cooked crab patties from the Air Fryer then serve. Enjoy immediately.

Halibut Cheesy Lemon

Servings: 6

Total Time: 45 Minutes

Calories: 346

Fat: 31.2 g

Protein: 15 g

Carbs: 1.1 g

Fiber: 3.4 g

Ingredients and Quantity

- 1 lb. halibut fillet
- 1/4 tsp. salt
- 1/4 tsp. pepper
- 1 tbsp. extra virgin olive oil
- 3/4 cup grated parmesan cheese
- 1/2 cup butter
- 2 1/2 tbsp. mayonnaise
- 2 1/2 tbsp. lemon juice
- 1/4 cup chopped onion

Direction

1. Brush the halibut fillet with olive oil then season with salt and pepper.
2. Preheat an Air Fryer to 375°F (191°C).
3. Once the Air Fryer is ready, place the seasoned halibut fillet in the Air Fryer and cook for 12 minutes.
4. Meanwhile, place butter in a mixing bowl then pours lemon juice over the butter.
5. Add mayonnaise to the mixing bowl then using an electric mixer beat the butter until smooth and creamy.
6. Next, stir in grated Parmesan cheese, and chopped onion then mixes well.
7. After 12 minutes of cooking time, open the drawer then spread the butter mixture over the cooked halibut.
8. Allow cooking for two minutes then remove from the Air Fryer.
9. Transfer the cooked halibut to a serving dish then serve. Enjoy right away.

Crispy Calamari with Lemon Butter

Servings: 8

Total Time: 20 Minutes

Calories: 429

Fat: 38.7 g

Protein: 16.3 g

Carbs: 8.2 g

Fiber: 4.2 g

Ingredients and Quantity

- 1 lb. fresh squids
- 1 tsp. salt
- 1 tsp. pepper
- 2 cup almond flour
- 1 cup water
- 1 cup butter
- 1 1/2 tbsp. mustard
- 2 tsp. lemon juice

Direction

1. Peel the outer skin of the squids then discard the ink.
2. Cut the squids into rings then rub with salt and pepper.
3. Roll the seasoned squids in the almond flour then dip in the water.
4. Return the squids to the almond flour then roll until the squids are completely coated with almond flour.
5. Preheat an Air Fryer to 400°F (204°C).
6. Place the coated squids in the Air Fryer then cook for 6 minutes.
7. Once it is done, remove from the Air Fryer then place on a serving dish.
8. Place butter in a mixing bowl then adds mustard and juice from the lemon.
9. Mix until smooth and fluffy.
10. Serve the fried calamari with the lemon butter. Enjoy!

Crispy Fried Tuna

Servings: 4

Total Time: 30 Minutes

Calories: 313

Fat: 28 g

Protein: 14.4 g

Carbs: 4.6 g

Fiber: 3.1 g

Ingredients and Quantity

- 1/2 lb. tuna steak
- 1 tbsp. lemon juice
- 1 egg
- 1 cup roasted pecans
- 1 tsp. ginger
- 1/2 tsp. chili powder
- 1/4 tsp. salt
- 1/4 tsp. pepper
- 1 tsp. extra virgin olive oil

Direction

1. Splash lemon juice over the tuna then let it rest for a few minutes.
2. Next, crack the egg then place in a bowl.
3. Season the egg with salt, pepper, and chili powder then stir until incorporated. Set aside.
4. Place roasted pecans in a food processor then process until becoming flour texture.
5. After that, add ginger to the pecans then process again until combined.
6. Transfer the pecans mixture to a bowl.
7. Mix the tuna in the egg mixture then roll in the pecan mixture.
8. Return to the egg mixture then roll again in the pecan mixture. Make sure that all sides of the tuna are completely coated with pecan.
9. Preheat an Air Fryer to 400°F (204°C) and place a rack in it.
10. Once the Air Fryer is ready, place the coated tuna on the rack then cook for 5 minutes.
11. Flip the tuna and cook again for another 5 minutes. The tuna will be lightly golden brown.
12. Remove the fried tuna from the Air Fryer then place in a serving dish. Serve and enjoy!

Fried Shrimps Garlic

Servings: 2

Total Time: 30 Minutes

Calories: 396

Fat: 31.5 g

Protein: 19.4 g

Carbs: 6.8 g

Fiber: 3.9 g

Ingredients and Quantity

- 1 lb. fresh shrimps
- 1/4 tsp. salt
- 1 tbsp. coriander

- 3 tbsp. minced garlic
- 1 tsp. extra virgin olive oil
- 1/4 cup butter
- 1 1/2 tsp. cayenne
- 1 tsp. smoked paprika
- 1 1/2 tbsp. Worcestershire sauce
- 2 tsp. lemon juice
- 1 tsp. ginger

Direction

1. Peel the shrimps then remove the head.
2. Season the shrimp with coriander, minced garlic, and salt. Let the shrimps rest for at least 10 minutes.
3. Place butter in a mixing bowl then adds cayenne, smoked paprika, Worcestershire sauce, ginger, and lemon juice.
4. Use an electric mixer to beat butter until it attains a creamy and smooth consistency. Set aside.
5. Preheat an Air Fryer to 400°F (204°C) and put a rack in it.
6. Place the seasoned shrimps on the rack then cook for 5 minutes.
7. Remove the cooked shrimps from the Air Fryer then serve with creamy hot butter. Enjoy!

Pork and Lamb Recipes

Lamb Sirloin Steak with Parsley Sauce

Servings: 8

Total Time: 60 Minutes

Calories: 358

Fat: 37.1 g

Protein: 5.1 g

Carbs: 3 g

Fiber: 3.5 g

Ingredients and Quantity

- 1 lb. lamb sirloin
- 1/2 cup chopped onion
- 3 tsp. ginger
- 4 tsp. minced garlic
- 1 1/2 tsp. fennel
- 1 1/2 tsp. cinnamon
- 3/4 tsp. cardamom
- 2 1/2 tsp. cayenne
- 3/4 tsp. salt
- 1 cup butter
- 1/4 cup chopped scallions
- 3 tsp. minced garlic
- 1/4 cup chopped parsley
- 3/4 tsp. chives
- 1 1/2 tsp. horseradish
- 1 1/4 tsp. thyme
- 3/4 tsp. paprika
- 1/4 tsp. pepper

Direction

1. Place chopped onion, ginger, garlic, fennel, cinnamon, cardamom, cayenne, and salt in a food processor. Process until smooth.
2. Cut the lamb sirloin into thin slices then rub with the spice mixture.
3. Marinate the lamb sirloin for at least 30 minutes.
4. After 30 minutes, preheat an Air Fryer to 400°F (204°C).
5. Place the seasoned sliced lamb in the Air Fryer then cook for 15 minutes.
6. Meanwhile, melt butter in a saucepan then stir in minced garlic to the saucepan. Sauté until aromatic.

7. Add scallions, parsley, chives, horseradish, thyme, paprika, and pepper then stir until thickened.
8. Get the sauce off heat then let it cool.
9. When the lamb is cooked, transfer to a serving dish.
10. Drizzle parsley sauce on top then serve.
11. Enjoy with roasted vegetables or any kinds of side dish, as you desire.

Spicy Lamb Satay

Servings: 3

Total Time: 60 Minutes

Calories: 249

Fat: 20.2 g

Protein: 12.9 g

Carbs: 3.7 g

Fiber: 2.4 g

Ingredients and Quantity

- 2 boneless lamb shoulders
- 1/2 tsp. salt
- 1/2 tsp. pepper
- 1 tsp. ginger
- 1/2 tsp. nutmeg
- 1/4 tsp. cumin
- 2 kaffir lime leaves
- 2 lemongrasses
- 1 tbsp. extra virgin olive oil

Direction

1. Place salt, pepper, ginger, nutmeg, and cumin in a bowl then mix well.
2. Cut the lamb shoulder into medium cubes then rub with the spice mixture.
3. Marinate the lamb cubes for 10 minutes then prick using steel skewers.
4. Preheat an Air Fryer to 400°F (204°C) and arrange the lamb satay in the Air Fryer.
5. Spray the lamb satay with olive oil then put lime leaves and lemon grasses on top.
6. Cook the lamb satay and set the time to 8 minutes.
7. Once it is done, remove from the Air Fryer and enjoy with any kind of low carb sauce, as you desire. Enjoy!

Pork Shoulder with Zucchini Salads

Servings: 2

Total Time: 60 Minutes

Calories: 372

... 35.1 g

Protein: 11.2 g

Carbs: 5.7 g

Fiber: 3.7 g

Ingredients and Quantity

- 1/2 pork shoulder
- 3 tbsp. extra virgin olive oil
- 2 tsp. salt
- 1 cup sliced zucchini
- 1/4 cup chopped onion
- 1/2 cup diced bell pepper
- 1 tbsp. chopped basil
- 1 tbsp. sesame oil
- 1 tbsp. lemon juice

Direction

1. Score the pork shoulder on several places then rub it with salt and olive oil. Repeat for three times.
2. Preheat an Air Fryer to 300°F (148°C).
3. Place the seasoned pork shoulder in the Air Fryer then cook for thirty minutes.
4. Once 30 minutes are over, increase the temperature to 400°F (204°C) and cook again for 20 minutes.
5. Meanwhile, place sliced zucchinis, chopped onion, diced bell pepper, and chopped basil in a salad bowl.
6. Sprinkle sesame oil and lemon juice over the salads then toss to combine. Store in the refrigerator.
7. Once the pork shoulder is done, remove from the Air Fryer and let it sit for about 10 minutes.
8. Cut into slices then arrange on a serving dish.
9. Serve with zucchini salads. Enjoy!

Pork Roast with Thai Walnuts Sauce

Servings: 2

Total Time: 45 Minutes

Calories: 325

Fat: 32.6 g

Protein: 6.7 g

Carbs: 3.2 g

Fiber: 3.2 g

Ingredients and Quantity

- 1 pork roast
- 1/2 tsp. salt

- 1 tbsp. extra virgin olive oil
- 1/2 tsp. pepper
- 1 tsp. thyme
- 1 tsp. rosemary
- 6 garlic cloves
- 1/2 cup butter
- 3 tbsp. roasted walnuts
- 3 tbsp. low sodium chicken broth
- 2 tbsp. lemon juice
- 1/2 tsp. ginger
- 2 tbsp. minced garlic

Direction

1. Place butter in a mixing bowl then adds roasted walnuts, ginger, and minced garlic.
2. Pour chicken broth and lemon juice into the mixing bowl then using an electric mixer beat until smooth.
3. Transfer the butter mixture to a container with a lid then store in a refrigerator overnight.
4. Preheat an Air Fryer to 350°F (177°C) and put garlic in the Air Fryer.
5. Brush the pork roast with olive oil then place in the Air Fryer after the garlic.
6. Sprinkle salt, pepper, thyme, and rosemary then cook for 30 minutes.
7. Once it is done, remove from the Air Fryer then place on a serving dish.
8. Serve with walnut sauce. Enjoy!

Spicy Glazed Pork Loaf

Servings: 8

Total Time: 40 Minutes

Calories: 255

Fat: 20.1 g

Protein: 13 g

Carbs: 6 g

Fiber: 2.5 g

Ingredients and Quantity

- 1 1/2 cup ground pork
- 1/2 cup diced pork rinds
- 1/2 tsp. paprika
- 1/2 tsp. pepper
- 2 tsp. minced garlic
- 1/2 cup chopped onion
- 1/2 tsp. cumin
- 1/2 tsp. cayenne
- 1/4 cup butter

- 1/2 cup tomato puree
- 1/2 tsp. chili powder
- 2 tbsp. coconut aminos
- 1/2 tsp. Worcestershire sauce
- 1 tsp. lemon juice

Direction

1. Combine ground pork and pork rinds in a bowl then season with paprika, pepper, minced garlic, cumin, cayenne, and chopped onion. Mix well.
2. Transfer the pork mixture to a silicone loaf pan then spread evenly. Set aside.
3. Next, melt the butter in microwave then set aside.
4. Combine the melted butter with tomato puree, chili powder, coconut aminos, Worcestershire sauce, and lemon juice. Stir until incorporated.
5. Drizzle the glaze mixture over the pork loaf then set aside.
6. Preheat an Air Fryer to 350°F (177°C).
7. Once the Air Fryer is preheated, place the silicon loaf pan on the Air Fryer's rack then cook for 20 minutes.
8. Remove from the Air Fryer then let it cool.
9. Cut the pork loaf into slices then serve. Enjoy!

Lamb Ribs with Minty Yogurt

Servings: 1

Total Time: 30 Minutes

Calories: 163

Fat: 15.3 g

Protein: 4.3 g

Carbs: 4.4 g

Fiber: 1.6 g

Ingredients and Quantity

- 1 lb. lamb ribs
- 1/2 tsp. salt
- 1/2 tsp. pepper
- 2 tbsp. mustard
- 1 tsp. chopped rosemary
- 1 cup Greek yogurt
- 1/4 cup chopped mint leaves

Direction

1. Brush mustard over the lamb ribs then sprinkles salt, pepper, and rosemary over the lamb.
2. Preheat an Air Fryer to 350°F (177°C).

3. Once the Air Fryer is ready, place the lamb ribs in the Air Fryer and set the time to 18 minutes.
4. In the meantime, combine yogurt with chopped mint leaves then stir well. Set aside.
5. Once the lamb ribs are done, remove from the Air Fryer and transfer to a serving dish.
6. Serve with minty yogurt then enjoy!

Note: This lamb ribs will be great to be enjoyed with roasted vegetables.

Baby Back Ribs Tender

Servings: 2

Total Time: 55 Minutes

Calories: 409

Fat: 34.3 g

Protein: 19.3 g

Carbs: 6.3 g

Fiber: 4 g

Ingredients and Quantity

- 2 baby back ribs
- 1/2 tsp. salt
- 3 tsp. grated garlic
- 3/4 tsp. ginger
- 3/4 tsp. pepper
- 2 tsp. red chili flakes
- 1 tbsp. extra virgin olive oil

Direction

1. Combine salt, grated garlic, ginger, pepper, and red chili flakes in a bowl then mix well.
2. Rub the baby back ribs with the spice mixture then set aside.
3. Preheat an Air Fryer to 350°F (177°C).
4. Place the seasoned baby back ribs and set the time to 30 minutes. Cook the baby back ribs.
5. Once it is done, remove from the Air Fryer then transfer to a serving dish.
6. Serve and enjoy immediately.

Lamb Curry in Wrap

Servings: 8

Total Time: 60 Minutes

Calories: 276

Fat: 21.8 g

Protein: 13.8 g

Carbs: 5.4 g

Fiber: 2.7 g

Ingredients and Quantity

- 1 lb. lamb loin
- 1 tbsp. extra virgin olive oil
- 1 cup chopped onion
- 2 tbsp. sliced shallots
- 1 cup chopped leek
- 1 tsp. curry powder
- 1/2 tsp. turmeric
- 1 tsp. black pepper
- 1/2 tsp. salt
- 1/4 cup coconut milk
- 1 cup coconut flour
- 3 egg yolks
- 2 cup water

Direction

1. Place the lamb loin a food processor then process until smooth.
2. Place the ground lamb in a bowl then add chopped onion, sliced shallots, and chopped leek to the bowl.
3. Season with curry powder, turmeric, salt, and pepper then pour a ½ tbsp. of olive oil and coconut milk to the bowl. Mix well.
4. Preheat an Air Fryer to 400°F (204°C).
5. Transfer the lamb mixture to the Air Fryer then cook for 15 minutes.
6. Meanwhile, combine coconut flour with egg yolks and water then stir until smooth and incorporated.
7. Using a saucepan make 8 thin omelets then set aside.
8. When the lamb is cooked through, transfer to a bowl.
9. Take a sheet of coconut flour omelet then place on a flat surface.
10. Drop 2 tbsp. of cooked lamb on the omelets then fold until becoming a tight roll.
11. Repeat with the remaining lamb and coconut flour omelet.
12. Preheat the Air Fryer again to 375°F (191°C).
13. Arrange the lamb rolls in the Air Fryer then spray with the remaining olive oil.
14. Cook the lamb rolls for 10 minutes then remove from the Air Fryer.
15. If you like the lamb rolls to be more golden brown, cook the lamb rolls for another 5 minutes. Serve and enjoy!

Veggies and Sides Recipes

Spinach in Cheese Envelopes

Servings: 8

Total Time: 45 Minutes

Calories: 365

Fat: 34.6 g

Protein: 10.4 g

Carbs: 4.4 g

Fiber: 3.6 g

Ingredients and Quantity

- 3 cups cream cheese
- 1 1/2 cup coconut flour
- 3 egg yolks
- 2 eggs
- 1/2 cup cheddar cheese
- 2 cup steamed spinach
- /4 tsp. salt
- 1/2 tsp. pepper
- 1/4 cup chopped onion

Direction

1. Place cream cheese in a mixing bowl, then whisk until soft and fluffy.
2. Add egg yolks to the mixing bowl, then continue whisking until well incorporated.
3. Stir in coconut flour to the cheese mixture, then mix until it becomes a soft dough.
4. Place the dough on a flat surface, then roll until thin.
5. Cut the thin dough into 8 squares, then keep.
6. Crack the eggs, then place in a bowl.
7. Season with salt, pepper and grated cheese, then mix well.
8. Add chopped spinach and onion to the egg mixture, then stir until well combined.
9. Put spinach filling on a square dough, then fold until it becomes an envelope.
10. Repeat with the remaining spinach filling and dough.
11. Glue with water.
12. Preheat an air fryer to 425 o F (218 o C).
13. Arrange the spinach envelopes in the air fryer and then cook for 12 minutes or until lightly golden brown.
14. Remove from the air fryer and serve warm. Enjoy!

Crispy Broccoli Pop Corn

Servings: 4

Total Time: 60 Minutes

Calories: 202

Fat: 17.5 g

Protein: 5.1 g

Carbs: 7.8 g

Fiber: 2 g

Ingredients and Quantity

- 2 cup broccoli florets
- 2 cup coconut flour
- 4 egg yolks
- 1/2 tsp. salt
- 1/2 tsp. pepper
- 1/4 cup butter

Direction

1. Soak the broccoli florets in salty water to remove all the insects inside.
2. Wash and rinse the broccoli florets then pat them dry.
3. Melt butter then let it cool.
4. Crack the eggs then place in the same bowl with the melted butter.
5. Add coconut flour to the liquid then season with salt and pepper. Mix until incorporated.
6. Preheat an Air Fryer to 400°F (204°C).
7. Dip a broccoli floret in the coconut flour mixture then place in the Air Fryer.
8. Repeat with the remaining broccoli florets.
9. Cook the broccoli florets 6 minutes. You may do this in several batches.
10. Once it is done, remove the fried broccoli popcorn from the Air Fryer then place on a serving dish.
11. Serve and enjoy immediately.

Cauliflower Florets in Curly Egg

Servings: 2

Total Time: 60 Minutes

Calories: 276

Fat: 21.8 g

Protein: 13.8 g

Carbs: 5.4 g

Fiber: 2.7 g

Ingredients and Quantity

- 2 cups cauliflower florets

- 3 tsp. minced garlic
- 1/2 tsp. salt
- 1/2 tsp. coriander
- 2 cups water
- 3 eggs
- 1/2 tsp. pepper
- 1/4 cup grated mozzarella cheese
- 2 tbsp. tomato puree

Direction

1. Place minced garlic, salt, and coriander in a container then pour water into it. Stir until the seasoning is completely dissolved.
2. Add the cauliflower florets to the brine then submerge for at least 30 minutes.
3. After 30 minutes, remove the cauliflower florets from the brine then wash and rinse them. Pat them dry.
4. Preheat an Air Fryer to 400°F (204°C).
5. Crash the eggs and place in a bowl.
6. Season with pepper, then whisk until well incorporated.
7. Dip a cauliflower floret in the egg, then place in the air fryer. Repeat with the remaining cauliflower florets and egg.
8. Cook the cauliflower florets for 12 minutes or until lightly golden and the egg is curly.
9. Sprinkle grated mozzarella cheese, then drizzle tomato puree on top.
10. Cook the cauliflower florets again for another 5 minutes and then remove from the air fryer.
11. Transfer to a serving dish and then serve warm. Enjoy!

Fried Green Beans Rosemary

Servings: 2

Total Time: 15 Minutes

Calories: 72

Fat: 6.3 g

Protein: 0.7 g

Carbs: 4.5 g

Fiber: 0.7 g

Ingredients and Quantity

- 3/4 cup chopped green beans
- 3 tsp. minced garlic
- 2 tbsp. rosemary
- 1/2 tsp. salt
- 1 tbsp. butter

Direction

1. Preheat an Air Fryer to 390°F (200°C).

2. Place the chopped green beans in the Air Fryer then brush with butter.
3. Sprinkle salt, minced garlic, and rosemary over the green beans then cook for 5 minutes.
4. Once the green beans are done, remove from the Air Fryer then place on a serving dish.
5. Serve and enjoy warm.

Cheesy Cauliflower Croquettes

Servings: 4

Total Time: 30 Minutes

Calories: 160

Fat: 13 g

Protein: 6.8 g

Carbs: 5.1 g

Fiber: 1.6 g

Ingredients and Quantity

- 2 cups cauliflower florets
- 2 tsp. minced garlic
- 1/2 cup chopped onion
- 3/4 tsp. mustard
- 1/2 tsp. salt
- 1/2 tsp. pepper
- 2 tbsp. butter
- 3/4 cup grated cheddar cheese

Direction

1. Place butter in a microwave-safe bowl then melts the butter. Let it cool.
2. Place cauliflower florets in a food processor then process until smooth and becoming crumbles.
3. Transfer the cauliflower crumbles to a bowl then add chopped onion and cheese.
4. Season with minced garlic, mustard, salt, and pepper then pour melted butter over the mixture.
5. Shape the cauliflower mixture into medium balls then arrange in the Air Fryer.
6. Preheat an Air Fryer to 400°F (204°C) and cook the cauliflower croquettes for 14 minutes.
7. To achieve a more golden brown color, cook the cauliflower croquettes for another 2 minutes.
8. Serve and enjoy with homemade tomato sauce.

HEALTHY LOW CARB AIR FRYER RECIPES

For weight watchers who have reached their weight loss target and wish to maintain their new body structure. Also for diabetic patients and those who wish to adopt a healthy feeding lifestyle.

Low Carb Air Fryer Breakfast Recipes

Fish Frittata

Servings: 3

Total Time: 25 Minutes

Calories: 211

Fat: 13 g

Protein: 22.5 g

Carbs: 1.7 g

Fiber: 0.4 g

Ingredients and Quantity

- 4 eggs
- 8 oz. salmon fillet, chopped
- 1 tbsp. fresh dill, chopped
- 1 tbsp. fresh parsley, chopped
- 1/4 tsp. ground nutmeg
- 2 tbsp. coconut milk

Direction

1. Beat the eggs in the mixing bowl and whisk well.
2. Add chopped salmon and fresh dill.
3. Add fresh parsley and ground nutmeg.
4. Stir the mixture gently and add coconut milk.
5. After this, pour the frittata mixture in the air fryer basket and cook for 15 minutes at 360 F.
6. When the meal is cooked – chill it little. Serve and enjoy!

Cherry Tomatoes Frittata

Servings: 2

Total Time: 25 Minutes

Calories: 234

Fat: 19.6 g

Protein: 11.9 g

Carbs: 5.4 g

Fiber: 2.2 g

Ingredients and Quantity

- 1/4 cup cherry tomatoes
- 1 tbsp. basil, chopped
- 3 eggs
- 2 tbsp. almond milk
- 1 tsp. olive oil
- 1/4 tsp. turmeric
- 1 tbsp. almond flour

Direction

1. Beat the eggs and whisk them well.
2. Add the chopped basil and almond milk.
3. Then add the almond flour and turmeric.
4. Stir the mixture well.
5. After this, cut the cherry tomatoes into the halves.
6. Pour the whisked egg mixture in the air fryer basket.
7. Add the cherry tomatoes.
8. Cook the frittata for 15 minutes at 355 F.
9. Then let the cooked frittata chill little. Serve and enjoy!

Whisked Eggs with Ground Chicken

Servings: 4

Total Time: 25 Minutes

Calories: 122

Fat: 6.6 g

Protein: 14.7 g

Carbs: 2.1 g

Fiber: 0.6 g

Ingredients and Quantity

- 3 eggs, whisked
- 1 cup ground chicken
- 1/2 tsp. salt

- 1 oz. fresh parsley, chopped
- 1/2 tsp. ground paprika
- 1/2 onion, chopped

Direction

1. Put the ground chicken in the air fryer basket.
2. Add salt, chopped parsley, and ground paprika.
3. After this, add the chopped onion and stir the mixture with the help of the wooden spatula.
4. Cook the ground chicken mixture for 8 minutes at 375 F.
5. Stir it time to time.
6. Then pour the whisked eggs over the ground chicken mixture and cook it for 7 minutes more at 365 F.
7. When the meal is cooked, stir it carefully and transfer in the serving bowls.
8. Serve it immediately. Enjoy!

Breakfast Bombs

Servings: 10

Total Time: 45 Minutes

Calories: 250

Fat: 45 g

Protein: 18 g

Carbs: 3.4 g

Fiber: 2 g

Ingredients and Quantity

- 1/4 lb. breakfast mini sausages
- 2 eggs, beat
- 1 tbsp. vegetable oil
- 1/8 tsp. salt
- 1/8 tsp. pepper
- 1 can refrigerated biscuits
- 2 oz. cheddar cheese
- For the Egg Wash:
- 1 egg
- 1 tbsp. water

Direction

1. Take two 8-inches round cut parchment papers.
2. Place one of these in air fryer basket and set it using cooking spray.
3. Heat oil to medium-high level in a nonstick pan and cook sausages for about 3 to 5 minutes.
4. Now reduce the heat to medium and add beaten eggs, pepper, and salt in the pan.
5. Cook until eggs are done and thick.
6. Keep stirring it to ensure moist and texture.

7. Separate the biscuit dough into biscuit sheets.
8. Assemble the mixture and top it with cheese on the dough.
9. Cover the sides and make it a ball.
10. Place the biscuit bombs in air fryer basket and top with the other parchment round sheet.
11. Cook the bombs for about 8 minutes at 325 degrees F.
12. Serve with sauce of your choice. Enjoy!

Baked Apples with Mixed Seeds

Servings: 4

Total Time: 15 Minutes

Calories: 105

Fat: 4 g

Protein: 45 g

Carbs: 8 g

Fiber: 3 g

Ingredients and Quantity

- 4 apples
- 25 g butter
- 2 tbsp. brown sugar
- 50 g fresh breadcrumbs
- 40 g mixed seeds
- Zest of 1 orange
- 1 tsp. cinnamon or mixed spice

Direction

1. Firstly, core the apples and score skin around circumference with the help of a sharp knife to stop them from splitting.
2. Carefully stuff the apple cores by combining all the remaining ingredients.
3. Bake in the air fryer at 180C for about 10 minutes until slightly collapsed. Serve and enjoy!

Parsnip Fries

Servings: 3

Total Time: 30 Minutes

Calories: 310

Fat: 5 g

Protein: 60 g

Carbs: 5 g

Fiber: 3 g

Ingredients and Quantity

- 2 to 3 medium size zucchini
- 1/4 cup cornstarch
- 2 tbsp. olive oil
- 1/4 cup water
- 1 pinch salt

Direction

1. Cut zucchini into 2 inches sticks.
2. In a medium bowl, mix cornstarch, olive oil, water and zucchini. Mix and coat zucchini evenly.
3. Place half of zucchini fries into the air fryer.
4. Cook for 12 to 14 minutes, until golden brown.
5. Repeat the process until all zucchinis are cooked.
6. Place the zucchini in plate. Serve and enjoy!

Corn on the Cob

Servings: 3

Total Time: 12 Minutes

Calories: 245

Fat: 9.5 g

Protein: 2.3 g

Carbs: 32 g

Fiber: 5.6 g

Ingredients and Quantity

- 3 corn on the cob
- Cooking spray
- Toppings
- 1 tbsp. lemon zest
- Salt, to taste
- 1 tbsp. cilantro

Direction

1. Preheat the fryer to 400 degrees F.
2. Put the corn on the cob in a bowl and mist with cooking spray to season with salt.
3. Cook the cob for about 10 minutes and keep flipping side in between.
4. Take out the corn on the cob and top with lemon zest, cilantro, and some extra salt. Serve and enjoy!

Chipotle Tuna Melt

Servings: 1

Total Time: 15 Minutes

Calories: 200

Fat: 12 g

Protein: 10 g

Carbs: 6.7 g

Fiber: 1 g

Ingredients and Quantity

- 2 slices Italian bread
- 1/2 cup mayonnaise
- 2 chipotle peppers in adobo sauce
- Pinch garlic salt
- Pinch black pepper
- Butter
- 12 oz. tuna
- Pinch cilantro
- 1 slice American cheese

Direction

1. Blend the Chipotle peppers in mayonnaise mixed with garlic salt, and black pepper.
2. Pour the mixture into a bowl and stir in the tuna.
3. In the same mixture, add cilantro and salt or pepper to taste.
4. Now, coat the toast with butter and spread the tuna on the buttered slice of bread.
5. Top with cheese and cover with the other slice of bread.
6. Butter the top slice as well.
7. Place the greased sandwich into the fryer basket and cook on 320 degrees for 5 minutes.
8. Remove from the basket when the cheese has completely melted and the toast is golden.
9. Serve with chips. Enjoy!

Baked Potatoes

Servings: 2

Total Time: 63 Minutes

Calories: 150

Fat: 13.4 g

Protein: 6 g

Carbs: 7.2 g

Fiber: 2 g

Ingredients and Quantity

- 2 slices Turkey bacon
- 2 tsp. sour cream
- 1 large, chopped green onion
- 2 tsp. butter
- 1/4 cup cheddar cheese, shredded
- 1 tsp. chives
- Salt, to taste
- Pepper, to taste

Direction

1. Take potatoes and poke holes in them with the help of fork.
2. Preheat Air-fryer at 350F.
3. Put poked potatoes in it and cook them for about 40 minutes until potatoes are cooked.
4. Take out the potatoes from air-fryer and let them cool.
5. Cut the potato half from mid horizontally.
6. Layer it with butter, put cheddar cheese, add salt and pepper to taste.
7. Top up the potatoes with sour cream, turkey bacon pieces, green onions and chives. Serve and enjoy!

Crumbled Fish

Servings: 7

Total Time: 20 Minutes

Calories: 256

Fat: 7 g

Protein: 12 g

Carbs: 10.3 g

Fiber: 3 g

Ingredients and Quantity

- 800 to 900 g white fish (like Atlantic Salmon)
- 2 eggs
- 2 tbsp. parmesan cheese
- 1/2 cup flour
- 1 cup bread crumbs
- Salt and pepper, to taste
- Cooking oil, for frying

Direction

1. After rinsing with water, dry fish with a paper towel.
2. Beat eggs lightly. Put some flour on one plate and bread crumbs on another.
3. Start heating your oil in a pan for frying.
4. Season your bread crumbs with salt and pepper.
5. Coat each piece of fish with the flour then in beaten egg and then in seasoned bread crumbs.
6. Deep fry the fish until it gets brown.
7. Drain it first on a paper towel so it can soak the excessive oil and then on a serving plate. Enjoy!

Strawberry Egg Rolls

Servings: 12

Total Time: 15 Minutes

Calories: 234

Fat: 4.6 g

Protein: 19 g

Carbs: 4 g

Fiber: 2.3 g

Ingredients and Quantity

- 12 sheets egg roll wrappers
- 1 tsp. vanilla extract
- 8 oz. softened cream cheese
- 1/2 cup sugar
- 1/2 cup sour cream
- 1 cup fresh strawberry
- Cooking spray
- Chocolate sauce, optional

Direction

1. Mix cream cheese, sugar, sour cream and vanilla extract in a mixture.
2. Dice strawberries into small pieces.
3. Take an egg sheet, fill in the cream cheese mixture and top it with strawberries.
4. Fold the sheet and close the roll using water on the seal.
5. Sprinkle cooking spray on rolls.
6. Cook them at 390 degrees F for about 5 minutes in the fryer.
7. Top with chocolate, strawberries and dust icing sugar. Serve and enjoy!

French Fries

Servings: 4

Total Time: 65 Minutes

Calories: 230

Fat: 10 g

Protein: 6 g

Carbs: 19 g

Fiber: 2 g

Ingredients and Quantity

- 1 kg floury potatoes
- 1 tbsp. olive oil

Direction

1. Peel the potatoes and cut into long fries, no more than 1cm thick.
2. In a bowl of cold, salted water, soak the fries for 30 minutes.
3. Drain and pat dry and toss with the olive oil.
4. Heat the Air fryer to 160C.
5. Place the fries in the basket and cook for no more than 15 minutes.
6. Shake the fries to turn them and raise the air fryer temperature to 180C and cook for 10 more minutes until golden brown. Serve and enjoy!

Breakfast Porridge

Servings: 2

Total Time: 14 Minutes

Calories: 169

Fat: 4.9 g

Protein: 3.7 g

Carbs: 29.8 g

Fiber: 4.5 g

Ingredients and Quantity

- 1 banana
- 1 egg, beaten
- 1 apple, chopped
- 1/2 tsp. ground cinnamon
- 1 tsp. olive oil
- 1 tsp. vanilla extract

Direction

1. Peel the banana and chop it into the small pieces.
2. Pour the olive oil into the air fryer basket.
3. Add the chopped apple.

4. Then sprinkle the apple with the ground cinnamon and banana.
5. Stir the mixture and add vanilla extract.
6. Then whisk the egg and pour it over the mixture. Stir it gently.
7. Cook the porridge for 7 minutes at 380 F.
8. When the porridge is cooked, let it chill little. Serve and enjoy!

Green Bacon Salad

Servings: 2

Total Time: 15 Minutes

Calories: 287

Fat: 22.7 g

Protein: 14.9 g

Carbs: 7.6 g

Fiber: 2.5 g

Ingredients and Quantity

- 1/4 cup fresh spinach
- 1/4 cup fresh parsley, chopped
- 1 red onion, chopped
- 1 tsp. olive oil
- 1 oz. walnuts, crushed
- 2 oz. bacon, chopped

Direction

1. Place the bacon in the air fryer basket and cook it for 5 minutes at 400 F. Stir it every 1 minute.
2. Meanwhile, chop the spinach and combine it together with the chopped parsley in the big bowl.
3. Add chopped onion and crushed walnuts.
4. After this, stir the mixture well.
5. Add the cooked hot bacon and stir the salad again.
6. Serve it immediately. Enjoy!

Hash with Eggs

Servings: 4

Total Time: 18 Minutes

Calories: 90

Fat: 5.8 g

Protein: 6.5 g

Carbs: 4 g

Fiber: 0.9 g

Ingredients and Quantity

- 1 zucchini
- 4 eggs
- 1/4 cup sweet corn
- 1/4 tsp. ground paprika
- 1 tsp. olive oil
- 1 tsp. dried dill
- 1/2 tsp. salt

Direction

1. Beat the eggs in the bowl and whisk them.
2. Add the dried dill and salt.
3. After this, chop the zucchini into the tiny pieces.
4. Put the zucchini in the air fryer basket.
5. Add olive oil and chopped zucchini.
6. Then add the whisked egg and stir the mixture gently.
7. Cook the hash for 8 minutes at 365 F.
8. When the time is over, stir the hash and check if it is cooked.
9. Serve it in the bowls. Enjoy!

Spaghetti Carrot Salad

Servings: 3

Total Time: 17 Minutes

Calories: 65

Fat: 1.1 g

Protein: 0.6 g

Carbs: 14.5 g

Fiber: 3 g

Ingredients and Quantity

- 2 carrots, peeled
- 1/2 tsp. olive oil
- 1 tsp. vinegar
- 1 apple
- 1 tsp. avocado oil
- 1/4 tsp. ground cinnamon

Direction

1. Make the spirals from the carrot with the help of the spiralizer.
2. After this, sprinkle the carrot spirals with the olive oil and place in the air fryer basket.

3. Cook the carrot spirals for 7 minutes at 365 F.
4. Stir the carrot every 2 minutes.
5. Place the cooked carrot spirals in the salad bowl.
6. Then chop the apple into the small cubes.
7. Add the apple to the salad bowl and sprinkle with the ground cinnamon and vinegar.
8. Add avocado oil and mix the salad up. Serve and enjoy!

Apple Bake

Servings: 3

Total Time: 20 Minutes

Calories: 252

Fat: 9.2 g

Protein: 4.2 g

Carbs: 43.1 g

Fiber: 7.8 g

Ingredients and Quantity

- 1 sweet potato, peeled
- 3 apples
- 3/4 cup pecans, chopped
- 1/2 tsp. ground cinnamon
- 1 tbsp. raisins
- 1 egg
- 1/4 cup coconut milk

Direction

1. Chop the sweet potato and apples into the same cubes.
2. Place them in the air fryer basket.
3. Add chopped pecans and ground cinnamon.
4. After this, add the raisins and coconut milk.
5. Whisk the egg in the bowl.
6. Pour the whisked egg over the air fryer mixture and stir gently with the help of the fork.
7. Cook the meal for 10 minutes at 390 F.
8. When the time is over, check if the apple bake is cooked and allow it rest for 10 minutes.
9. After this, serve and enjoy!

Apple Salad with Tuna

Servings: 2

Total Time: 18 Minutes

Calories: 305

Fat: 10.6 g

Protein: 24.3 g

Carbs: 29 g

Fiber: 5.2 g

Ingredients and Quantity

- 1 sweet potato, chopped
- 1 apple
- 1 tbsp. avocado oil
- 6 oz. tuna, canned
- 1/4 red onion, chopped
- 1 tsp. vinegar
- 1 tsp. olive oil
- 1/4 tsp. sesame seeds

Direction

1. Place the chopped sweet potato in the air fryer.
2. Sprinkle it with the vinegar and red chopped onion.
3. Add the olive oil and shake it gently.
4. Cook the vegetables for 8 minutes at 400 F.
5. After this, stir the vegetables and chill them little.
6. Chop the apple and place it in the bowl.
7. Add canned tuna and sesame seeds.
8. After this, add avocado oil and cooked vegetables.
9. Mix the salad carefully. Serve and enjoy!

Zucchini Noodles Salad

Servings: 4

Total Time: 21 Minutes

Calories: 72

Fat: 4.4 g

Protein: 1.6 g

Carbs: 7.6 g

Fiber: 2.7 g

Ingredients and Quantity

- 1 zucchini
- 1 carrot
- 1 tsp. flax seeds

- 1 tbsp. coconut flour
- 1 tbsp. olive oil
- 1 tsp. vinegar
- 1 sweet pepper
- 1/4 tsp. chili flakes

Direction

1. Spiralize the zucchini and carrot and place them in the air fryer basket.
2. Add coconut flour, vinegar, and olive oil.
3. Then sprinkle the vegetables with the chili flakes and cook for 6 minutes at 400 F. The vegetables should be a little bit soft.
4. Meanwhile, cut the sweet pepper into the strips.
5. Place the pepper in the bowl and add the cooked spiralized vegetables.
6. Then add the flax seeds and all the remaining liquid from the vegetables that were cooked in the air fryer.
7. Stir the salad. Serve and enjoy!

Egg in Bacon Wholes

Servings: 2

Total Time: 25 Minutes

Calories: 373

Fat: 28.3 g

Protein: 26.8 g

Carbs: 1.5 g

Fiber: 0.9 g

Ingredients and Quantity

- 2 eggs
- 6 bacons slices
- 1/4 tsp. oregano
- 1/4 tsp. ground paprika
- 1 tbsp. parsley, chopped

Direction

1. Take the small ramekins and place the bacon slices in them by crosses.
2. Sprinkle the bacon with the oregano and ground paprika.
3. Then beat the eggs over the bacon.
4. Place the ramekins in the air fryer basket.
5. Cook the breakfast for 15 minutes at 360 F or until the eggs are just right.
6. Then sprinkle the eggs with the chopped parsley. Serve and enjoy!

Eggs in Carrot Nests

Servings: 3

Total Time: 23 Minutes

Calories: 93

Fat: 5.9 g

Protein: 5.9 g

Carbs: 4.5 g

Fiber: 1.1 g

Ingredients and Quantity

- 2 carrots
- 1/4 tsp. ground black pepper
- 3/4 tsp. salt
- 3 eggs
- 1 tsp. olive oil

Direction

1. Peel the carrots and grate them.
2. Sprinkle the grated carrot with the ground black pepper, cilantro, and salt.
3. Stir the vegetables and add olive oil.
4. Stir the carrot well.
5. Make the medium nests from the grated carrot in the ramekins.
6. Place the ramekins in the air fryer basket and cook for 5 minutes at 380 F.
7. After this beat the eggs over the carrot nests.
8. Cook the eggs for 8 minutes more at 275 F.
9. When the eggs are cooked, serve them immediately. Enjoy!

Eggs in Mushroom Hats

Servings: 2

Total Time: 18 Minutes

Calories: 187

Fat: 10.7 g

Protein: 8.7 g

Carbs: 14.7 g

Fiber: 2.1 g

Ingredients and Quantity

- 2 Portobello mushrooms (hats)

- 2 eggs
- 1 tsp. fresh dill
- 1 tsp. fresh parsley
- 1/4 tsp. salt
- 1 tsp. olive oil

Direction

1. Combine together the fresh dill, parsley, salt, and olive oil.
2. Stir the mixture until homogenous.
3. Then sprinkle the mushroom hats with the green mixture.
4. Beat the eggs in the bowl and whisk well.
5. Place the mushroom hats in the air fryer basket.
6. Then pour the whisked egg inside the mushroom hats.
7. Cook the mushrooms for 8 minutes at 390 F.
8. When the meal is cooked, let it chill for 3 minutes. Serve and enjoy!

Tuna Salad

Servings: 2

Total Time: 20 Minutes

Calories: 252

Fat: 10.7 g

Protein: 29 g

Carbs: 10.1 g

Fiber: 3.1 g

Ingredients and Quantity

- 5 oz. broccoli, chopped
- 1 onion, chopped
- 7 oz. tuna, canned
- 1 tsp. olive oil
- 1/4 tsp. minced garlic
- 2 tsp. Paleo mayonnaise
- 1 tbsp. fresh parsley, chopped

Direction

1. Place the broccoli, onion, minced garlic, and olive oil in the air fryer basket.
2. Stir the vegetable mixture.
3. Cook it at 380 F for 10 minutes.
4. Stir the vegetables during cooking 2 times.
5. Then chop the tuna and put it in the bowl.
6. Add Paleo mayonnaise and chopped fresh parsley.

7. Add cooked vegetables and stir carefully. Serve and enjoy!

Chicken Sausage

Servings: 6

Total Time: 18 Minutes

Calories: 189

Fat: 9.5 g

Protein: 23.9 g

Carbs: 1.4 g

Fiber: 0.7 g

Ingredients and Quantity

- 1 pound ground chicken
- 1 tsp. ground paprika
- 1 egg
- 1/2 tsp. minced garlic
- 1/4 tsp. ground nutmeg
- 1 tbsp. almond flour
- 1 tsp. olive oil

Direction

1. Beat the egg in the mixing bowl.
2. Whisk it and add ground paprika, minced garlic, ground nutmeg, and almond flour.
3. Stir the mixture until homogenous.
4. After this, add the ground chicken and stir it carefully with the help of the spoon.
5. Make the medium sausages from the mixture with the help of the hands.
6. Pour the olive oil in the air fryer basket.
7. Place the sausages in the air fryer basket carefully.
8. Cook the sausages for 8 minutes at 390 F.
9. Turn the sausages into another side after 4 minutes of cooking.
10. Then chill the cooked sausages little. Serve and enjoy!

Egg Bowl

Servings: 4

Total Time: 26 Minutes

Calories: 118

Fat: 8.1 g

Protein: 6.7 g

Carbs: 6.4 g

Fiber: 1.1 g

Ingredients and Quantity

- 4 eggs
- 2 cucumber, chopped
- 3/4 tsp. ground black pepper
- 3/4 tsp. ground paprika
- 1 tsp. olive oil
- 1 tbsp. chives
- 1 tbsp. fresh parsley, chopped
- 1 tsp. vinegar

Direction

1. Place the eggs on the air fryer rack and cook them for 16 minutes at 250 F.
2. Meanwhile, put the chopped cucumbers in the big bowl.
3. Add chives and fresh parsley.
4. After this, combine together the olive oil, ground paprika, and ground black pepper.
5. Add vinegar and stir the mixture until homogenous.
6. When the eggs are cooked, chill them in the ice water and peel.
7. Chop the eggs and add them to the bowl too.
8. Stir the mixture with the help of 2 forks.
9. Then sprinkle it with the oil dressing. Serve and enjoy!

Quail Eggs in Mushrooms

Servings: 3

Total Time: 20 Minutes

Calories: 85

Fat: 5.7 g

Protein: 7.1 g

Carbs: 2.4 g

Fiber: 0.6 g

Ingredients and Quantity

- 5 oz. mushrooms
- 3 quail eggs
- 3/4 tsp. olive oil
- 3/4 tsp. minced garlic
- 1 tsp. fresh parsley, chopped
- 2/3 tsp. oregano

Direction

1. Mix up together the olive oil, minced garlic, chopped parsley, and oregano.
2. Stir the mixture well.
3. Brush the mushrooms with the oil mixture carefully.
4. Then beat the eggs in the hats and transfer in the air fryer basket.
5. Cook the mushrooms for 10 minutes at 380 F. Check the mushrooms after 6 minutes of cooking – reduce the temperature if needed.
6. Chill the cooked breakfast for 5 minutes. Serve and enjoy!

Basil-Spinach Quiche

Servings: 4

Total Time: 20 Minutes

Calories: 237

Fat: 21.8 g

Protein: 8.7 g

Carbs: 5.3 g

Fiber: 2.4 g

Ingredients and Quantity

- 1/2 cup spinach
- 1 oz. fresh basil, chopped
- 1 oz. walnuts
- 3 eggs
- 3/4 cup almond milk
- 1/2 tsp. salt
- 1 tbsp. almond flour

Direction

1. Chop the spinach and combine it together with the chopped basil.
2. Crush the walnuts and add them to the green mixture too.
3. After this, add the salt and almond flour.
4. Stir the mixture and place it in the air fryer basket.
5. Then beat the eggs in the separate bowl and whisk well.
6. Add almond milk and stir carefully.
7. Pour the egg mixture over the greens and cook it for 10 minutes. at 375 F.
8. When the quiche is cooked, let it chill well. Serve and enjoy!

Eggs on Avocado Burgers

Servings: 2

Total Time: 25 Minutes

Calories: 361

Fat: 31 g

Protein: 310.8 g

Carbs: 15 g

Fiber: 9 g

Ingredients and Quantity

- 1 avocado, pitted
- 2 eggs
- 1 tbsp. almond flour
- 1 oz. onion, chopped
- 1/2 carrot, grated
- 1/2 tsp. salt
- 1/4 tsp. ground black pepper

Direction

1. Peel the avocado and mash it.
2. Add the almond flour and grated carrot in the mashed avocado mixture.
3. Then add salt and ground black pepper.
4. After this, mix the mixture until homogenous.
5. Make the small burgers from the mixture.
6. Pour the olive oil in the air fryer basket and add the avocado burgers.
7. Cook them for 8 minutes at 375 F.
8. Flip them into another side after 4 minutes of cooking.
9. Transfer the cooked burgers on the plates.
10. After this, beat the eggs in the air fryer basket and cook them for 7 minutes at 360 F or until you get cooked eggs.
11. Put the eggs over the avocado burgers. Serve immediately. Enjoy!

Beef Balls with Sesame and Dill

Servings: 4

Total Time: 20 Minutes

Calories: 207

Fat: 10.7 g

Protein: 24.7 g

Carbs: 2.7 g

Fiber: 1.1 g

Ingredients and Quantity

- 1 tsp. sesame seeds
- 1 tbsp. dill, dried
- 1 egg
- 10 oz. ground beef
- 1 garlic clove, chopped
- 3/4 tsp. nutmeg
- 1 tsp. olive oil
- 1 tsp. almond flour

Direction

1. Beat the egg in the bowl and whisk it.
2. Add dried dill and sesame seeds.
3. Stir gently and add chopped garlic clove and nutmeg.
4. Then add ground beef and almond flour.
5. Mix the mixture carefully with the help of the spoon.
6. Pour the olive oil in the air fryer basket.
7. Make the medium balls from the meat mixture and place them in the air fryer.
8. Cook the meatballs for 10 minutes at 380 F.
9. Stir the meatballs during the cooking with the help of the wooden spatula.
10. Transfer the cooked meatballs in the serving bowls. Serve and enjoy!

Zucchini Rounds with Ground Chicken

Servings: 4

Total Time: 23 Minutes

Calories: 143

Fat: 6.6 g

Protein: 18.5 g

Carbs: 2.1 g

Fiber: 0.8 g

Ingredients and Quantity

- 8 oz. ground chicken
- 1 zucchini
- 1 egg
- 1/4 tsp. ground black pepper
- 1/2 tsp. salt
- 1 tsp. paprika
- 1 tsp. olive oil
- 1 tsp. cilantro

Direction

1. Beat the egg in the bowl and whisk well.
2. Add the ground black pepper, salt, paprika, and cilantro.
3. Add ground chicken and stir the mixture.
4. Cut zucchini into 4 rounds and remove the meat from them to make the zucchini circles.
5. Then place the zucchini circles in the air fryer basket.
6. Fill the zucchini with the ground chicken mixture.
7. Cook the breakfast for 8 minutes at 360 F.
8. When the meal is cooked, let it chill for 5 minutes. Serve and enjoy!

Tomatoes with Chicken

Servings: 3

Total Time: 25 Minutes

Calories: 78

Fat: 3.1 g

Protein: 7.9 g

Carbs: 5.1 g

Fiber: 1.5 g

Ingredients and Quantity

- 3 tomatoes
- 1/2 cup ground chicken
- 1 tsp. Paleo mayonnaise
- 1/4 tsp. turmeric
- 3/4 tsp. minced garlic
- 1 tsp. chives

Direction

1. Cut the "hats" in every tomato.
2. Then remove the meat from the tomatoes to get the tomato cups.
3. Mix up together the minced garlic, chives, turmeric, mayonnaise and ground chicken in the mixing bowl.
4. Stir the mixture.
5. After this, fill tomato cups with the ground chicken mixture and place them in the air fryer basket.
6. Cook the tomatoes for 10 minutes at 365 F.
7. When the time is over, check of the tomatoes is cooked and remove them from the air fryer.
8. Chill the tomatoes with chicken gently. Serve and enjoy!

Meatball Salad

Servings: 2

Total Time: 25 Minutes

Calories: 208

Fat: 14.9 g

Protein: 7.9 g

Carbs: 5.1 g

Fiber: 2.1 g

Ingredients and Quantity

- 1 cucumber, chopped
- 1 tomato, chopped
- 1 sweet red pepper, chopped
- 1/2 cup ground chicken
- 1 egg
- 1 tbsp. olive oil
- 2/3 tsp. minced garlic
- 1/2 tsp. ground black pepper

Direction

1. Put the cucumber, tomato, and sweet red pepper in the mixing bowl.
2. Add olive oil and stir gently.
3. After this, mix up together the ground black pepper, minced garlic, and ground chicken.
4. Beat the egg in the chicken mixture and stir well. Make the medium meatballs.
5. After this, place the ground chicken meatballs in the air fryer basket and cook it for 10 minutes at 375 F.
6. Stir the ground chicken meatballs time to time.
7. Then chill the meatballs and add them in the salad.
8. Serve the breakfast immediately. Enjoy!

Applesauce Mash with Sweet Potato

Servings: 4

Total Time: 12 Minutes

Calories: 94

Fat: 1.4 g

Protein: 0.9 g

Carbs: 21.3 g

Fiber: 3.7 g

Ingredients and Quantity

- 1 sweet potato, peeled
- 2 apples
- 3/4 tsp. salt
- 1 tsp. olive oil

Direction

1. Grate the sweet potatoes and apples.
2. Place the grated ingredients in the air fryer basket.
3. Add salt and olive oil.
4. Stir the mixture with the help of the wooden spatula.
5. Cook the applesauce for 7 minutes at 390 F.
6. When the applesauce is cooked- let it chill little. Serve and enjoy!

Bacon and Kale Salad

Servings: 6

Total Time: 15 Minutes

Calories: 232

Fat: 16.6 g

Protein: 14.5 g

Carbs: 6.4 g

Fiber: 1.3 g

Ingredients and Quantity

- 7 oz. bacon, sliced
- 10 oz. kale, chopped
- 1 tsp. olive oil
- 1/4 cup almonds, crushed
- 1/2 tsp. paprika
- 1/2 tsp. salt

Direction

1. Place the bacon in the air fryer and sprinkle it with the paprika and salt.
2. Cook the bacon for 5 minutes at 400 F. Stir it after 3 minutes of cooking.
3. Meanwhile, place the kale in the salad bowl.
4. Add the olive oil and crushed almonds.
5. When the bacon is cooked – chop it roughly and add in the kale bowl.
6. Shake it gently. Serve and enjoy!

Kale Quiche with Eggs

Servings: 6

Total Time: 28 Minutes

Calories: 166

Fat: 11.8 g

Protein: 7.7 g

Carbs: 8.5 g

Fiber: 1.8 g

Ingredients and Quantity

- 1 cup kale
- 3 eggs
- 2 oz. bacon, chopped, cooked
- 1 sweet potato, grated
- 1/2 tsp. thyme
- 1/2 tsp. ground black pepper
- 1/2 tsp. ground paprika
- 1/2 cup coconut milk
- 1 onion, chopped
- 1 tsp. olive oil

Direction

1. Chop the kale roughly and place it in the blender.
2. Blend it gently.
3. Then transfer the blended kale in the mixing bowl.
4. Add the grated potato and thyme.
5. Sprinkle the mixture with the ground black pepper and ground paprika.
6. Add coconut milk and chopped onion.
7. Pour the olive oil into the air fryer basket.
8. Then place the kale mixture in the air fryer basket.
9. Beat the eggs in the separate bowl and whisk well.
10. Pour the whisked eggs over the kale mixture. Add bacon.
11. Cook the quiche for 18 minutes at 350 F.
12. When the time is over – chill the quiche little. Serve and enjoy!

Bacon Hash

Servings: 2

Total Time: 29 Minutes

Calories: 168

Fat: 8.5 g

Protein: 5.8 g

Carbs: 18.7 g

Fiber: 3.5 g

Ingredients and Quantity

- 1 oz. bacon, chopped

- 1 carrot
- 1 apple
- 1 tsp. olive oil
- 1/2 tsp. salt
- 1/4 tsp. thyme

Direction

1. Put the chopped bacon in the air fryer basket.
2. Add salt and stir it gently.
3. Cook the bacon for 4 minutes at 365 F.
4. Peel the carrot and grate it.
5. Add the grated carrot.
6. Then grate the apple and add the carrot mixture too.
7. Stir it carefully.
8. Sprinkle the bacon hash with the thyme and stir gently again.
9. Cook the bacon hash for 15 minutes at 365 F.
10. Stir it carefully. Serve and enjoy!

Eggs in Avocado

Servings: 2

Total Time: 17 Minutes

Calories: 268

Fat: 24 g

Protein: 7.5 g

Carbs: 9 g

Fiber: 6.7 g

Ingredients and Quantity

- 1 avocado, pitted
- 2 eggs
- 1/2 ground black pepper
- 3/4 tsp. salt

Direction

1. Cut the avocado into the halves.
2. Then sprinkle the avocado with the black pepper and salt.
3. Beat the eggs and place them in the avocado halve's wholes.
4. Place the avocado in the air fryer basket.
5. Cook the meal for 7 minutes at 380 F.
6. When the eggs are cooked – the meal is ready to eat.
7. Serve it immediately. Enjoy!

Bacon and Zucchini Latkes

Servings: 4

Total Time: 20 Minutes

Calories: 102

Fat: 7.7 g

Protein: 6.1 g

Carbs: 3.4 g

Fiber: 1.3 g

Ingredients and Quantity

- 1 zucchini
- 1 oz. bacon, chopped
- 1 egg
- 1 tbsp. almond flour
- 1/4 tsp. paprika

Direction

1. Grate the zucchini and put it in the mixing bowl.
2. Beat the egg in the grated zucchini and stir the mixture until homogenous.
3. After this, add the almond flour and paprika. Stir the mixture.
4. Preheat the air fryer.
5. Then make the medium latkes with the help of the spoon and place them in the preheated air fryer.
6. Cook the latkes for 4 minutes from each side at 400 F.
7. Serve the cooked meal immediately. Enjoy!

Meat Bagels

Servings: 4

Total Time: 22 Minutes

Calories: 207

Fat: 9.6 g

Protein: 25.5 g

Carbs: 4.3 g

Fiber: 1.4 g

Ingredients and Quantity

- 11 oz. ground beef
- 1 onion, grated
- 1/2 tsp. salt

- 1 tsp. almond flour
- 1 tsp. minced garlic
- 1 tsp. olive oil

Direction

1. Place the ground beef in the mixing bowl.
2. Add the grated onion and salt.
3. After this, add the almond flour and minced garlic.
4. Mix the mixture carefully until homogenous.
5. Then make the medium bagels from the ground beef.
6. Pour the olive oil in the air fryer basket.
7. Then place the meat bagels in the air fryer basket and cook them for 6 minutes from each side at 380 F.
8. Chill the meat bagels gently. Serve and enjoy!

Egg Muffins with Greens

Servings: 4

Total Time: 25 Minutes

Calories: 109

Fat: 8.9 g

Protein: 6.3 g

Carbs: 1.8 g

Fiber: 0.7 g

Ingredients and Quantity

- 1/4 cup almond flour
- 4 eggs
- 1/2 tsp. salt
- 3/4 tsp. ground paprika
- 1 tbsp. chives
- 1/4 cup tbsp. milk

Direction

1. Beat the egg in the bowl and whisk them carefully.
2. Add the salt and ground paprika.
3. After this, add the almond milk and chives. Stir the mixture.
4. Add the almond flour and stir the egg mixture.
5. Pour the egg mixture in the muffin molds and place them in the air fryer basket.
6. Cook the meal for 10 minutes at 370 F.
7. Let the cooked muffins chill little. Serve and enjoy!

Spaghetti Squash Casserole Cups

Servings: 2

Total Time: 25 Minutes

Calories: 119

Fat: 3.2 g

Protein: 4.7 g

Carbs: 20.1 g

Fiber: 1.9 g

Ingredients and Quantity

- 12 oz. spaghetti squash
- 1 carrot, grated
- 1 egg
- 1/3 tsp. chili flakes
- 1 onion, chopped

Direction

1. Peel the spaghetti squash and grate it.
2. Mix up together the spaghetti squash and carrot.
3. Beat the egg and stir it carefully.
4. After this, add the chili flakes and chopped onion. Stir it.
5. Place the mixture in the air fryer basket and cook the casserole for 15 minutes at 365 F.
6. When the casserole is cooked, chill it till the room temperature. Serve and enjoy!

Bacon Wrapped Chicken Fillet

Servings: 6

Total Time: 30 Minutes

Calories: 310

Fat: 19.5 g

Protein: 31.1 g

Carbs: 0.8 g

Fiber: 0.1 g

Ingredients and Quantity

- 15 oz. chicken fillet
- 6 oz. bacon, sliced
- 1/2 tsp. salt
- 1 tsp. paprika

- 1 tbsp. olive oil
- 1 garlic clove, chopped

Direction

1. Rub the chicken fillet with the salt, paprika, garlic clove and olive oil.
2. Wrap the rubbed chicken fillet in the bacon and secure gently with the toothpicks.
3. Place the chicken fillets in the air fryer basket.
4. Cook the chicken for 15 minutes at 380 F.
5. Stir the chicken every 5 minutes.
6. Then slice the cooked chicken fillet. Serve and enjoy!

Egg Whites with Sliced Tomatoes

Servings: 2

Total Time: 25 Minutes

Calories: 45

Fat: 2.5 g

Protein: 4 g

Carbs: 1.9 g

Fiber: 0.5 g

Ingredients and Quantity

- 1 tomato, sliced
- 2 egg whites
- 1/4 tsp. ground paprika
- 1/4 tsp. salt
- 1 tsp. olive oil
- 1 tsp. dried dill

Direction

1. Pour the olive oil in the air fryer.
2. Then add the egg whites.
3. Sprinkle the egg whites with the salt, dried dill, and ground paprika.
4. Cook the egg whites for 15 minutes at 350 F.
5. When the egg whites are cooked – let them chill little.
6. Place the layer of the sliced tomatoes on the plate.
7. Then chop the egg whites roughly and place over the tomatoes. Serve and enjoy!

Whole Food Eggs in Burgers

Servings: 2

Total Time: 33 Minutes

Calories: 223

Fat: 12.1 g

Protein: 26.1 g

Carbs: 1.7 g

Fiber: 0.8 g

Ingredients and Quantity

- 1 cup ground chicken
- 2 eggs
- 1 tsp. olive oil
- 1 tsp. coconut flour
- 1 tsp. dried basil
- 1 tsp. dried oregano

Direction

1. Place the ground chicken in the mixing bowl.
2. Add coconut flour, dried basil, and dried oregano. Stir the mixture.
3. Make the medium balls from the meat mixture and flatten them gently in the shape of the burgers.
4. Then pour the olive oil into the air fryer basket.
5. Place the burgers in the air fryer and make the holes in the center of every burger.
6. Beat the eggs in the burger wholes.
7. Cook the burgers for 18 minutes at 360 F.
8. When the burgers are cooked, transfer them to the serving plate. Serve and enjoy!

Bacon Sandwich with Guacamole

Servings: 4

Total Time: 21 Minutes

Calories: 416

Fat: 35.5 g

Protein: 16.2 g

Carbs: 10.4 g

Fiber: 7.1 g

Ingredients and Quantity

- 2 avocado
- 1 tomato, chopped
- 1/4 onion, chopped
- 1/4 fresh cilantro, chopped
- 8 bacon slices

Direction

1. Place the sliced bacon in the air fryer basket.
2. Cook the bacon for 6 minutes at 400 F.
3. Flip the bacon on another side after 3 minutes.
4. Meanwhile, peel the avocados and mash them until smooth.
5. Add chopped onion and tomato.
6. After this, add the chopped cilantro and stir the mixture until homogenous and smooth.
7. When the bacon is cooked – chill it little.
8. After this, spread 4 bacon slices with the avocado mixture and make the sandwiches with the remaining bacon.
9. Serve immediately. Enjoy!

Bacon and Egg Muffins

Servings: 4

Total Time: 35 Minutes

Calories: 250

Fat: 18.3 g

Protein: 16.9 g

Carbs: 4.4 g

Fiber: 1 g

Ingredients and Quantity

- 1 onion, diced
- 4 oz. diced
- 4 eggs
- 1/4 cup almond flour
- 1/4 tsp. ground black pepper
- 1 tomato, chopped
- 1 tsp. olive oil

Direction

1. Beat the eggs and whisk well.
2. Chop the bacon and add it to the egg mixture.
3. After this, add almond flour, ground black pepper, and chopped tomato.
4. Then add the diced onion.
5. Stir it carefully until homogenous.
6. Spray the muffin molds with the olive oil.
7. After this, pour the egg mixture into the muffin molds.
8. Transfer the muffins molds in the air fryer basket.
9. Cook the muffins for 20 minutes at 350 F.
10. Then chill the muffins and discard them from the muffin molds. Serve and enjoy!

Apple Bowl with Ground Cinnamon

Servings: 2

Total Time: 17 Minutes

Calories: 191

Fat: 2.9 g

Protein: 1.3 g

Carbs: 45.2 g

Fiber: 7.5 g

Ingredients and Quantity

- 2 apples, chopped
- 1 tsp. ground cinnamon
- 1 banana, chopped
- 1 tsp. olive oil

Direction

1. Place the olive oil in the air fryer basket and preheat at 400 F for 2 minutes.
2. Then add the chopped apples and sprinkle with the ground cinnamon.
3. Stir carefully and cook for 3 minutes at 400 F.
4. Then stir the apples and add the chopped banana.
5. Stir the mix gently and cook for 2 minutes more.
6. Chill the cooked apple mixture for 5 minutes. Serve and enjoy!

Low Carb Air Fryer Main Dish Recipes

Tomato Beef Brisket

Servings: 6

Total Time: 65 Minutes

Calories: 175

Fat: 7.5 g

Protein: 24.7 g

Carbs: 1.1 g

Fiber: 0.4 g

Ingredients and Quantity

- 17 oz. beef brisket
- 1/2 cup tomato
- 1 cup fresh basil
- 1 tsp. cayenne pepper
- 1 tbsp. olive oil
- 1 tsp. turmeric

Direction

1. Put the tomatoes in the blender and blend them well.
2. Add fresh basil and blend the mixture until smooth.
3. After this, pour the tomato mixture over the beef brisket.
4. Sprinkle it with the cayenne pepper, olive oil, and turmeric and stir carefully.
5. Let it marinate for 20 minutes.
6. Then place the beef brisket in the air fryer basket and cook it at 370 F for 30 minutes. Stir the beef every 5 minutes.
7. When the meat is cooked, let it chill for 5 minutes. Serve and enjoy!

Spicy Meat Bowl

Servings: 6

Total Time: 31 Minutes

Calories: 289

Fat: 21.5 g

Protein: 21.7 g

Carbs: 1.3 g

Fiber: 0.3 g

Ingredients and Quantity

- 1 cup ground pork
- 8 oz. bacon, chopped
- 1 tbsp. chives
- 1 tsp. salt
- 1/2 tsp. ground black pepper
- 1/2 tsp. minced garlic
- 1/4 tsp. chili flakes
- 1 tbsp. olive oil
- 1/4 cup almond milk

Direction

1. Pour the olive oil into the air fryer basket.
2. Add ground pork, chopped bacon, chives, salt, ground black pepper, minced garlic, chili flakes, and almond milk.
3. Stir the mixture well and cook it at 380 F for 16 minutes. Stir the meat every 5 minutes.
4. When the meat is cooked, stir it one more time. Serve and enjoy!

Stuffed Sweet Potato

Servings: 6

Total Time: 20 Minutes

Calories: 145

Fat: 7.9 g

Protein: 16.7 g

Carbs: 1.3 g

Fiber: 0.4 g

Ingredients and Quantity

- 3 sweet potatoes
- 6 tsp. almond milk
- 1 tsp. minced garlic
- 12 oz. ground chicken
- 1 tsp. chives
- 1 tbsp. olive oil
- 1 tbsp. turmeric
- 1 tsp. avocado oil

Direction

1. Cut the sweet potatoes into the halves and remove the meat.

2. Then mix up together the almond milk, minced garlic, ground chicken, chives, olive oil, and turmeric. Stir the mixture.
3. Sprinkle the sweet potato halves with the avocado oil.
4. Then fill the sweet potatoes with the meat mixture and wrap them in foil.
5. Place the sweet potatoes in the air fryer basket and cook at 380 F for 30 minutes.
6. When the time is over, discard the foil from the sweet potatoes. Serve and enjoy!

Thyme Flank Steak

Servings: 4

Total Time: 23 Minutes

Calories: 213

Fat: 11 g

Protein: 26.7 g

Carbs: 0.5 g

Fiber: 0.3 g

Ingredients and Quantity

- 17 oz. flank steak
- 1 tbsp. thyme
- 11 tbsp. olive oil
- 1/2 tsp. salt
- 1 tsp. chili flakes

Direction

1. Rub the flank beef steak with the thyme, salt, and chili flakes.
2. Then sprinkle the meat with the olive oil on both sides.
3. Place the flank steak in the air fryer and cook it for 13 minutes at 400 F.
4. Flip the steak into another side after 7 minutes of cooking.
5. Serve the cooked flank steak immediately. Enjoy!

Turkey Meatballs

Servings: 4

Total Time: 20 Minutes

Calories: 261

Fat: 16.7 g

Protein: 30.3 g

Carbs: 1.7 g

Fiber: 0.8 g

Ingredients and Quantity

- 2 cups ground turkey
- 1 egg beaten
- 1 tbsp. almond flour
- 1/2 tsp. minced garlic
- 1/2 tsp. cilantro, dried
- 1 tsp. olive oil

Direction

1. Combine together the beaten egg and ground turkey.
2. Add almond flour and minced garlic.
3. After this, add the dried cilantro and mix the mixture carefully until homogenous.
4. Preheat the air fryer to 400 F.
5. Then pour the olive oil into the air fryer basket.
6. Make the medium meatballs from the mixture and place them in the air fryer.
7. Cook the meatballs for 10 minutes at 380 F.
8. Stir the meatballs after 5 minutes of cooking.
9. Serve the cooked meal immediately. Enjoy!

Turkey Hash

Servings: 3

Total Time: 22 Minutes

Calories: 216

Fat: 11.3 g

Protein: 27.2 g

Carbs: 5.9 g

Fiber: 1.6 g

Ingredients and Quantity

- 10 oz. ground turkey
- 1 tsp. chili flakes
- 1/2 tsp. turmeric
- 1 tsp. salt
- 1/2 tsp. cayenne pepper
- 1 sweet pepper, chopped
- 1 tbsp. avocado oil
- 1 zucchini, chopped

Direction

1. Pour the avocado oil in the air fryer.

2. Add the ground turkey, chili flakes, turmeric, and salt.
3. Stir the ground turkey mixture and cook at 380 F for 5 minutes.
4. After this, add chopped zucchini and sweet pepper.
5. Stir the hash and cook it for 12 minutes at 400 F. Stir the meal time to time.
6. When the turkey hash is cooked, let it chill little. Serve and enjoy!

Stuffed Peppers

Servings: 2

Total Time: 35 Minutes

Calories: 253

Fat: 10.6 g

Protein: 31.6 g

Carbs: 7.3 g

Fiber: 1.6 g

Ingredients and Quantity

- 1 big sweet pepper, halved
- 1 cup ground beef
- 1 tomato, chopped
- 1 garlic clove, chopped
- 1/2 tsp. salt
- 1/2 tsp. ground black pepper
- 1/2 tsp. turmeric
- 1 tbsp. coconut milk
- 1 tsp. olive oil

Direction

1. Remove the seeds from the pepper halves.
2. Then mix up together the ground beef, chopped tomato, garlic clove, salt, ground black pepper, turmeric, and coconut milk.
3. Mix the mixture carefully with the help of the spoon.
4. Then fill the pepper halves with the ground beef mixture and sprinkle them with the olive oil.
5. Transfer the stuffed pepper halves in the air fryer basket and cook them for 20 minutes at 360 F.
6. Check if the stuffed peppers are cooked and serve them immediately. Enjoy!

Whole Garlic Chicken

Servings: 13

Total Time: 1 Hour 15 Minutes

Calories: 286

Fat: 11.8 g

Protein: 40.8 g

Carbs: 1.9 g

Fiber: 0.2 g

Ingredients and Quantity

- 4 pounds whole chicken
- 1/2 cup garlic cloves
- 1 tsp. ground coriander
- 1/2 tsp. cayenne pepper
- 1/2 tsp. turmeric
- 1 tsp. ground paprika
- 1 tsp. salt
- 1 tbsp. olive oil
- 1 tsp. coconut oil

Direction

1. Chop the garlic cloves and combine them together with the ground coriander, cayenne pepper, turmeric, ground paprika, salt, coconut oil, and olive oil.
2. Stir the mixture until homogenous.
3. Then rub the chicken with the spice mixture generously.
4. Put the whole chicken in the air fryer basket and cook it for 60 minutes at 360 F.
5. When the chicken is cooked, chill it a bit. Serve and enjoy!

Pork Chops

Servings: 6

Total Time: 25 Minutes

Calories: 278

Fat: 22.3 g

Protein: 18.1 g

Carbs: 0.3 g

Fiber: 0.2 g

Ingredients and Quantity

- 17 oz. pork chops
- 1 tbsp. olive oil
- 1/2 tsp. ground paprika
- 1 tsp. ground black pepper
- 1/2 tsp. salt

Direction

1. Sprinkle the pork chops with the ground paprika, ground black pepper, and salt.
2. Then sprinkle the meat with the olive oil and massage it carefully from both sides with the help of the hands.
3. Place the pork chops in the air fryer basket and cook them for 15 minutes at 390 F.
4. Stir the pork chops time to time.
5. Serve the cooked meat immediately. Enjoy!

Chimichurri Chicken

Servings: 4

Total Time: 18 Minutes

Calories: 158

Fat: 7.9 g

Protein: 19.9 g

Carbs: 0.7 g

Fiber: 0.3 g

Ingredients and Quantity

- 12 oz. chicken wings
- 1/2 cup fresh parsley
- 1 tsp. ground black pepper
- 1 tbsp. vinegar
- 1 tbsp. lemon juice
- 1/2 tsp. salt
- 1 tbsp. olive oil

Direction

1. Sprinkle the chicken wings with the ground black pepper, vinegar, lemon juice, salt, and olive oil.
2. Shake the chicken wings well and transfer to the air fryer basket.
3. After this, cook the chicken wings for 10 minutes at 390 F. Stir them time to time.
4. Then sprinkle the chicken wings with the fresh chopped parsley and cook for 2 minutes more.
5. Serve the chicken immediately. Enjoy!

Lamb Burger

Servings: 6

Total Time: 35 Minutes

Calories: 271

Fat: 11.2 g

Protein: 39.8 g

Carbs: 0.3 g

Fiber: 0.1 g

Ingredients and Quantity

- 10 oz. lamb fillet
- 1 tsp. thyme
- 1/2 tsp. minced garlic
- 1/2 tsp. ground paprika
- 1/2 tsp. salt
- 1 tsp. olive oil

Direction

1. Chop the lamb fillet into the tiny pieces.
2. Sprinkle the meat with the thyme, minced garlic, ground paprika, and salt.
3. Stir it carefully until homogenous.
4. After this, make the medium burgers from the lamb meat mixture.
5. Pour the olive oil in the air fryer basket and add the lamb burgers.
6. Cook the lamb burgers for 20 minutes (10 minutes from each side) at 375 F. Serve and enjoy!

Parsley Meatballs

Servings: 3

Total Time: 20 Minutes

Calories: 122

Fat: 6.7 g

Protein: 14.9 g

Carbs: 0.2 g

Fiber: 0.1 g

Ingredients and Quantity

- 1 tbsp. fresh parsley, chopped
- 1 tsp. dried parsley
- 1 cup ground pork
- 1/4 tsp. cayenne pepper
- 1/2 tsp. salt
- 1 tbsp. olive oil

Direction

1. Blend the chopped parsley and combine it together with the dried parsley, ground pork, cayenne pepper, and salt.
2. Mix the mixture up and make the medium meatballs.

3. Spray the air fryer with the olive oil.
4. Add the meatballs and cook them for 10 minutes at 380 F. Stir the meatballs half-way.
5. Serve the cooked meatballs immediately. Enjoy!

Paprika Beef Short Ribs

Servings: 8

Total Time: 38 Minutes

Calories: 250

Fat: 12.1 g

Protein: 32.9 g

Carbs: 0.5 g

Fiber: 0.3 g

Ingredients and Quantity

- 2 pound beef short ribs
- 1 tsp. salt
- 1 tbsp. ground paprika
- 1 tsp. cilantro
- 1/2 tsp. basil, dried
- 1 tbsp. olive oil

Direction

1. Sprinkle the ribs with the salt, ground paprika, cilantro, basil, and olive oil.
2. Stir the meat carefully and leave for 10 minutes to marinate.
3. After this, put the beef short ribs in the air fryer and cook at 400 F for 18 minutes.
4. Stir the meat every 4 minutes.
5. Then transfer the cooked short ribs in the serving bowl.
6. Best served hot. Enjoy!

Whole Food Chili

Servings: 4

Total Time: 40 Minutes

Calories: 52

Fat: 1.2 g

Protein: 2.8 g

Carbs: 8.8 g

Fiber: 2.1 g

Ingredients and Quantity

- 1 cup ground beef
- 1 tbsp. avocado oil
- 1 sweet pepper, chopped
- 1 red onion, chopped
- 3 garlic cloves, chopped
- 1/4 tsp. cumin
- 1 tsp. cayenne pepper
- 1/2 tsp. chili pepper
- 2 tomatoes, chopped
- 1 cup beef broth
- 1 tsp. salt

Direction

1. Place the ground beef in the air fryer basket and add avocado oil.
2. Cook the meat for 5 minutes at 400 F.
3. Then add the chopped sweet pepper, onion, garlic clove, cumin, cayenne pepper, chill pepper, chopped tomato, beef broth and salt.
4. Stir the chili and cook for 25 minutes at 375 F.
5. When the chili is cooked, let it rest for 15 minutes. Serve and enjoy!

Lime Chicken with Pistachio

Servings: 4

Total Time: 27 Minutes

Calories: 206

Fat: 11.1 g

Protein: 24.9 g

Carbs: 1.7 g

Fiber: 0.7 g

Ingredients and Quantity

- 1 pound chicken breast, boneless
- 1/4 cup pistachios, crushed
- 1 tbsp. avocado oil
- 1/4 lime
- 2 tbsp. Paleo mayo
- 1/4 cup chicken stock

Direction

1. Squeeze the juice from the lime.
2. Sprinkle the chicken breast with the lime juice.

3. Then rub the chicken with Paleo mayo and crushed pistachios.
4. Place the chicken in the air fryer basket and sprinkle with the avocado oil.
5. Cook the chicken for 10 minutes at 365 F.
6. After this, add the chicken stock and cook the chicken for 7 minutes more at 375 F.
7. When the chicken is cooked, let it chill little. Serve and enjoy!

Turkey Dill Meatballs

Servings: 6

Total Time: 16 Minutes

Calories: 337

Fat: 19.8 g

Protein: 43.7 g

Carbs: 2.2 g

Fiber: 0.8 g

Ingredients and Quantity

- 2 pounds ground turkey
- 1/4 cup fresh dill
- 1 egg
- 1 tbsp. almond flour
- 1 tsp. salt

Direction

1. Blend the dill in the blender until smooth.
2. Then beat the egg in the blended dill and combine it with the almond flour, salt, and ground turkey.
3. Mix the mixture carefully with the help of the spoon.
4. After this, make the small meatballs.
5. Place the meatballs in the air fryer basket and cook them for 3 minutes from each side at 400 F.
6. Then chill the meatballs. Serve and enjoy!

Basil Beef Shank

Servings: 4

Total Time: 45 Minutes

Calories: 244

Fat: 10.7 g

Protein: 34.6 g

Carbs: 0.6 g

Fiber: 0.3 g

Ingredients and Quantity

- 1 pound beef shank
- 1 tsp. paprika
- 1 tsp. chili flakes
- 1 tbsp. olive oil
- 1/2 cup fresh basil
- 1 tsp. minced garlic

Direction

1. Sprinkle the beef shank with the paprika, chili flakes, and minced garlic.
2. Combine together the fresh basil and olive oil.
3. Blend it and rub the beef shank with the green mixture.
4. Transfer the beef shank in the air fryer and cook it for 30 minutes at 380 F. Stir the meat time to time.
5. When the time is over, check if the meat is cooked and serve it immediately. Enjoy!

Lime Chicken Breast

Servings: 4

Total Time: 35 Minutes

Calories: 171

Fat: 6.4 g

Protein: 24.4 g

Carbs: 3.3 g

Fiber: 1.1 g

Ingredients and Quantity

- 1 pound chicken breast
- 1 lime
- 1 tsp. ground paprika
- 1 tsp. turmeric
- 1 tsp. thyme
- 1 tsp. cilantro
- 1 tsp. ground black pepper
- 1/4 tsp. ground cinnamon
- 1 garlic clove, chopped
- 1/4 cup water
- 1 tbsp. coconut oil

Direction

1. Chop the lime into the tiny pieces.

2. Place the lime in the bowl and add ground paprika, turmeric, thyme, cilantro, ground black pepper and ground cinnamon.
3. Add chopped garlic clove and coconut oil.
4. Stir the mixture carefully until homogenous.
5. Then rub the chicken breast with the lime mixture generously.
6. Place the chicken breast in the air fryer basket and add water.
7. Cook the chicken for 25 minutes at 380 F.
8. When the meat is cooked, chill it. Serve and enjoy!

Tuna Casserole

Servings: 4

Total Time: 35 Minutes

Calories: 301

Fat: 22.8 g

Protein: 15.9 g

Carbs: 11.5 g

Fiber: 4 g

Ingredients and Quantity

- 1 can tuna
- 2 oz. celery, chopped
- 1 onion, diced
- 1 carrot, chopped
- 1 zucchini, spiralized
- 1 cup coconut milk
- 1 tsp. salt
- 1/2 tsp. ground black pepper
- 1/2 tsp. cilantro
- 1 tsp. turmeric
- 1 tsp. olive oil
- 1 tbsp. almond flour

Direction

1. Chop the tuna and put it in the air fryer basket.
2. Then combine together the diced onion, chopped carrot, spiralized zucchini, salt, ground black pepper, cilantro and turmeric.
3. Add olive and almond flour.
4. Stir the vegetables and place them over the trout.
5. Add coconut milk and cook the casserole for 20 minutes at 380 F.
6. When the casserole is cooked, let it rest little. Serve and enjoy!

Buffalo Chicken Casserole

Servings: 5

Total Time: 30 Minutes

Calories: 221

Fat: 14.2 g

Protein: 16.6 g

Carbs: 6.8 g

Fiber: 2.6 g

Ingredients and Quantity

- 4 tbsp. buffalo sauce
- 1 tsp. salt
- 1/2 tsp. ground black pepper
- 1/2 tsp. paprika
- 12 oz. chicken breast, boneless
- 1 egg white, whisked
- 1 onion, chopped
- 1 tsp. oregano
- 1 tsp. olive oil
- 1 cup almond milk

Direction

1. Combine together salt, ground black pepper, paprika, oregano, and olive oil.
2. Add almond milk and stir the mixture.
3. Then add chopped onion and whisked the egg.
4. Chop the chicken breast and place it in the air fryer basket.
5. Sprinkle the chicken with buffalo sauce and add the almond milk mixture.
6. Cook the chicken for 20 minutes at 360 F.
7. When the meal is cooked, chill it little. Serve immediately. Enjoy!

Bacon Chicken Thighs

Servings: 4

Total Time: 45 Minutes

Calories: 261

Fat: 21.3 g

Protein: 15.8 g

Carbs: 0.8 g

Fiber: 0.1 g

Ingredients and Quantity

- 4 chicken thighs
- 6 oz. bacon, sliced
- 1/4 tsp. turmeric
- 1/3 tsp. oregano
- 1/2 tsp. dried basil
- 1 tbsp. olive oil
- 1 tsp. chili flakes

Direction

1. Mix up together the turmeric, oregano, dried basil, olive oil, and chili flakes.
2. Stir the mixture and rub the chicken thighs with it.
3. Leave the chicken for 10 minutes to marinate.
4. Place the bacon in air fryer basket.
5. Then place the chicken thighs over the bacon and cook the meal for 25 minutes at 380 F.
6. When the chicken is cooked, transfer it with the cooked bacon in the serving plates. Serve and enjoy!

Orange Chicken

Servings: 6

Total Time: 30 Minutes

Calories: 242

Fat: 7.6 g

Protein: 33.8 g

Carbs: 8.6 g

Fiber: 2.2 g

Ingredients and Quantity

- 2 pound chicken breast, boneless
- 2 oranges
- 1 tsp. coconut oil
- 1 tbsp. almond flour
- 1 tbsp. almond milk
- 1/2 tsp. cayenne pepper
- 1/2 tsp. salt
- 1 tsp. paprika

Direction

1. Chop the oranges and place them in the big bowl.
2. Add chicken breast.
3. Then sprinkle the meat with the almond milk and almond flour.

4. Add cayenne pepper, salt, and paprika.
5. Stir the meat carefully and place it in the air fryer.
6. Cook the chicken breast for 20 minutes at 380 F. Stir the chicken time to time.
7. Transfer the cooked chicken breast in the serving bowls with the chopped oranges and almond milk liquid. Serve and enjoy!

Lemon Trout

Servings: 4

Total Time: 22 Minutes

Calories: 248

Fat: 13.1 g

Protein: 30.3 g

Carbs: 0.7 g

Fiber: 0.2 g

Ingredients and Quantity

- 1 pound trout
- 1/2 lemon
- 1/4 tsp. chili flakes
- 1/2 tsp. salt
- 1/2 tsp. ground coriander
- 1 tbsp. coriander
- 1 tbsp. olive oil
- 1 tbsp. basil

Direction

1. Slice the lemon.
2. Rub the fish with the chili flakes, salt, ground coriander, basil, and olive oil carefully.
3. Then fill the fish with the sliced lemon and transfer it to the air fryer basket.
4. Cook the trout for 12 minutes at 375 F.
5. When the trout is cooked, serve it hot. Enjoy!

Stuffed Salmon Fillet with Tomatoes

Servings: 6

Total Time: 30 Minutes

Calories: 222

Fat: 11.7 g

Protein: 29.5 g

Carbs: 0.5 g

Fiber: 0.1 g

Ingredients and Quantity

- 2 pounds salmon fillet
- 1 tsp. minced garlic
- 1/4 cup fresh basil
- 1/4 cup cherry tomatoes
- 1 tbsp. olive oil
- 1/2 tsp. dried dill

Direction

1. Blend the fresh basil until smooth.
2. Then sprinkle the salmon fillet with the dried dill, olive oil, and minced garlic.
3. Make the cut in the salmon fillet and fill it with the blended basil and cherry tomatoes.
4. Secure the cut with the toothpicks if desired.
5. Place the salmon in the air fryer basket and cook it for 15 minutes at 385 F.
6. When the salmon is cooked, serve it only hot. Enjoy!

Garlic Pork Chops

Servings: 5

Total Time: 28 Minutes

Calories: 324

Fat: 25.4 g

Protein: 20.7 g

Carbs: 2.2 g

Fiber: 0.5 g

Ingredients and Quantity

- 16 oz. pork chops
- 1 tbsp. olive oil
- 1/2 tsp. minced garlic
- 1 tsp. dried basil
- 1/2 tsp. oregano
- 1 onion, sliced

Direction

1. Pour olive oil in the air fryer basket.
2. Then beat the pork chops gently and sprinkle them with the minced garlic, dried basil, and oregano.
3. Place the pork chops in the air fryer and cook them for 10 minutes at 400 F.

4. Flip the meat to another side after 5 minutes of cooking.
5. Then add the sliced onion and cook the meat for 3 minutes more at the same temperature.
6. Serve the cooked pork chops immediately. Enjoy!

Chicken Drumsticks with Spinach Sauce

Servings: 4

Total Time: 35 Minutes

Calories: 234

Fat: 11.9 g

Protein: 30 g

Carbs: 0.7 g

Fiber: 0.4 g

Ingredients and Quantity

- 15 oz. chicken drumsticks
- 1 cup fresh spinach
- 1 tbsp. olive oil
- 1/2 tsp. minced garlic
- 1 tbsp. walnuts
- 1 tsp. coconut oil
- 1/2 tsp. thyme

Direction

1. Pour the coconut oil into the air fryer basket.
2. Sprinkle the chicken drumsticks with the minced garlic and thyme and place them in the air fryer basket.
3. Cook the chicken for 5 minutes at 400 F. Stir it frequently.
4. Meanwhile, blend together the fresh spinach, olive oil, and walnuts.
5. Transfer the blended mixture over the drumsticks and cook them for 15 minutes at 370 F.
6. When the time is over and the chicken drumsticks are cooked, allow them chill little. Serve and enjoy!

Sesame Pork Cubes

Servings: 4

Total Time: 25 Minutes

Calories: 291

Fat: 17 g

Protein: 32.1 g

Carbs: 1.1 g

Fiber: 0.6 g

Ingredients and Quantity

- 1 tbsp. avocado oil
- 16 oz. pork fillet
- 1 tbsp. sesame seeds
- 1 tsp. group black pepper
- 1 tsp. Paleo mayo

Direction

1. Chop the pork fillet into the cubes.
2. Sprinkle the pork cubes with the ground black pepper and Paleo mayo. Stir the meat.
3. Then add avocado oil and stir it one more time.
4. After this, place the meat in the air fryer basket and cook it for 10 minutes at 370 F.
5. Then stir the meat and add sesame seeds.
6. Cook the meat for 5 minutes more at 365 F.
7. When the meat is cooked, let it chill little. Serve and enjoy!

Thai Chicken

Servings: 4

Total Time: 25 Minutes

Calories: 246

Fat: 13.8 g

Protein: 25.8 g

Carbs: 4.7 g

Fiber: 1.2 g

Ingredients and Quantity

- 12 oz. chicken fillet
- 1 tbsp. curry
- 1 oz. lemongrass
- 1/2 cup almond milk
- 3/4 cup chicken stock
- 1/2 tsp. salt
- 1 tsp. minced garlic

Direction

1. Chop the chicken fillet roughly.
2. Then sprinkle the chicken with the curry, salt, and minced garlic.
3. Stir the meat and place it in the air fryer basket.
4. Add almond milk and lemongrass.
5. Cook the chicken for 15 minutes at 380 F.

6. When Thai chicken is cooked, let it chill little. Serve and enjoy!

Mango Turkey

Servings: 3

Total Time: 23 Minutes

Calories: 232

Fat: 12.2 g

Protein: 26.5 g

Carbs: 8.4 g

Fiber: 1.2 g

Ingredients and Quantity

- 5 oz. mango, chopped
- 10 oz. ground turkey
- 1/4 cup onion, grated
- 1/2 tsp. salt
- 1 tsp. olive oil
- 1 tsp. paprika

Direction

1. Place the chopped mango in the air fryer basket.
2. Add grated onion, salt, paprika, and olive oil.
3. Stir the mango mixture and cook it for 5 minutes at 375 F.
4. Then stir the mango mixture and add the ground turkey.
5. Stir the mixture well and cook it for 10 minutes at 375 F. Stir the meal frequently.
6. Transfer the cooked turkey to the serving bowl. Serve and enjoy!

Turkey Burger with Jalapeno

Servings: 4

Total Time: 30 Minutes

Calories: 208

Fat: 11.9 g

Protein: 25.8 g

Carbs: 2.5 g

Fiber: 1.5 g

Ingredients and Quantity

- 13 oz. ground turkey

- 1 jalapeno
- 1 tsp. olive oil
- 1 tbsp. coconut flour
- 1/2 tsp. paprika
- 1/4 tsp. nutmeg
- 1 tbsp. chives

Direction

1. Chop the jalapeno and blend it.
2. Combine together jalapeno and ground turkey.
3. Add coconut flour, paprika, nutmeg, and chives.
4. Stir the mixture well and make the medium burgers.
5. Place the burgers in the air fryer basket and spray them with the olive oil.
6. Cook the burgers for 15 minutes at 375 F.
7. When the burger are cooked, chill them little. Serve and enjoy!

Fennel Fish Fillet

Servings: 4

Total Time: 25 Minutes

Calories: 225

Fat: 9.8 g

Protein: 28.5 g

Carbs: 4.5 g

Fiber: 1.9 g

Ingredients and Quantity

- 1 pound whit fish fillet
- 8 oz. fennel
- 1/2 tsp. sea salt
- 1 tbsp. vinegar
- 1 tsp. ground black pepper
- 1 tsp. olive oil

Direction

1. Chop the fennel roughly.
2. Chop the white fish and place it in the air fryer.
3. Sprinkle the fish with the sea salt, vinegar, ground black pepper, and olive oil.
4. Stir the fish gently with the help of the spatula.
5. Cook the white fish for 5 minutes at 400 F.
6. Then add the chopped fennel and stir the fish.
7. Cook the fish for 10 minutes more at 360 F.

8. When the meal is cooked, transfer it directly to the serving plate. Serve and enjoy!

Ground Beef Bowl

Servings: 4

Total Time: 25 Minutes

Calories: 236

Fat: 8.5 g

Protein: 35 g

Carbs: 3.3 g

Fiber: 1 g

Ingredients and Quantity

- 2 tbsp. chives
- 1 onion, chopped
- 16 oz. ground beef
- 1 tsp. olive oil
- 1 tsp. paprika
- 1 tsp. cumin
- 1/2 tsp. ground black pepper

Direction

1. Put the ground beef in the air fryer basket.
2. Sprinkle the meat with the cumin, paprika, ground black pepper, and olive oil.
3. Stir it and cook for 7 minutes at 380 F. Stir the meat time to time.
4. After this, add chopped onion and chives.
5. Stir the meat mixture and cook it at 380 F for 8 minutes more or until all the ingredients are cooked.
6. Transfer the ground beef to the bowl. Serve and enjoy!

Turmeric Chicken Liver

Servings: 5

Total Time: 17 Minutes

Calories: 250

Fat: 26.1 g

Protein: 35 g

Carbs: 3.4 g

Fiber: 1.2 g

Ingredients and Quantity

- 17 oz. chicken liver
- 2 tbsp. almond flour
- 1 tbsp. coconut oil
- 1/2 tsp. salt
- 1/4 tsp. minced garlic
- 3/4 cup chicken stock

Direction

1. Place the coconut oil in the air fryer basket and preheat it for 20 seconds.
2. Then add chicken liver.
3. Stir it and cook for 2 minutes at 400 F.
4. Then sprinkle the chicken liver with the almond flour, salt, and minced garlic.
5. Add the chicken stock and stir liver and cook it for 5 minutes more or until cooked.
6. Serve the meal immediately. Enjoy!

Cabbage Soup

Servings: 4

Total Time: 30 Minutes

Calories: 134

Fat: 4.4 g

Protein: 16.4 g

Carbs: 7.3 g

Fiber: 2.6 g

Ingredients and Quantity

- 4 cups water
- 10 oz. cabbage, shredded
- 7 oz. ground beef
- 1 garlic clove, chopped
- 1 tsp. olive oil
- 1 onion, diced
- 1/2 tsp. salt
- 1/2 tsp. ground black pepper
- 1 tsp. dried oregano

Direction

1. Combine together the dried oregano, ground black pepper, salt, chopped garlic clove and ground beef in the mixing bowl.
2. Stir the mixture.
3. After this, place the mixture in the air fryer basket and add the olive oil.
4. Stir the mixture and cook it for 5 minutes at 390 F.

5. After this, add the shredded cabbage and water.
6. Then add the diced onion and cook the soup for 15 minutes at 370 F.
7. When the soup is cooked, all the ingredients should be soft.
8. Let the soup rest little. Serve and enjoy!

Thai Soup

Servings: 2

Total Time: 25 Minutes

Calories: 374

Fat: 31.7 g

Protein: 5.6 g

Carbs: 24.2 g

Fiber: 7 g

Ingredients and Quantity

- 1 tsp. curry powder
- 1 cup coconut milk
- 1 cup chicken stock
- 4 oz. broccoli florets
- 1/2 tsp. salt
- 1/2 apple, chopped
- 1 onion, diced
- 1/2 tsp. ground coriander
- 1 tsp. olive oil

Direction

1. Combine together curry powder and coconut milk.
2. Stir it carefully.
3. Then add chicken stock.
4. Pour the mixture in the air fryer basket and cook it for 5 minutes at 400 F.
5. After this, add the broccoli florets and diced onion.
6. Add the chopped apples and salt.
7. Then sprinkle the soup with the ground coriander and olive oil.
8. Cook it for 10 minutes at 350 F.
9. When the soup is cooked, serve it hot. Enjoy!

Whole Food Green Soup

Servings: 4

Total Time: 17 Minutes

Calories: 92

Fat: 2.6 g

Protein: 7.1 g

Carbs: 11 g

Fiber: 2.2 g

Ingredients and Quantity

- 1 cup spinach
- 1/2 cup dill
- 1/4 cup parsley
- 4 cups beef broth
- 1 tsp. salt
- 1 tbsp. almond milk
- 1 sweet potato, peeled
- 1/2 tsp. minced garlic

Direction

1. Place the spinach in the blender.
2. Add dill and parsley.
3. Blend the mixture until smooth.
4. Then transfer the green mixture in the air fryer basket.
5. Add beef broth and salt.
6. Sprinkle the mixture with the almond milk and minced garlic.
7. Grate the sweet potato and add it to the mixture.
8. Cook the soup for 7 minutes at 390 F.
9. When the soup is cooked, you can blend it with the hand blender to make the texture smooth. Serve and enjoy!

Beef and Broccoli Bowl

Servings: 4

Total Time: 36 Minutes

Calories: 142

Fat: 5.9 g

Protein: 17.5 g

Carbs: 5.8 g

Fiber: 1.5 g

Ingredients and Quantity

- 7 oz. broccoli florets
- 14 oz. beef fillet

- 1/2 tsp. salt
- 1/2 tsp. paprika
- 1/2 tsp. turmeric
- 1/2 tsp. thyme
- 1 tsp. olive oil
- 1 tbsp. fresh lemon juice
- 1 tsp. minced garlic

Direction

1. Chop the beef and sprinkle it with the salt, paprika, turmeric, thyme, lemon juice, and olive oil.
2. Add the minced garlic and stir the meat carefully.
3. Place the beef in the air fryer basket and cook it for 20 minutes at 360 F.
4. Stir it time to time.
5. After this, add the broccoli florets and cook the meal for 6 minutes more at 400 F.
6. When the meal is cooked, stir it carefully and transfer to a serving bowl. Serve and enjoy!

White Chicken Chili

Servings: 5

Total Time: 40 Minutes

Calories: 261

Fat: 7.3 g

Protein: 29.5 g

Carbs: 18.1 g

Fiber: 2.9 g

Ingredients and Quantity

- 15 oz. chicken fillet
- 1 onion, diced
- 1 tsp. minced garlic
- 1/4 tsp. cayenne pepper
- 1/4 tsp. salt
- 2 potatoes, peeled
- 1 sweet pepper
- 1/4 cup fresh cilantro, chopped
- 3 cups chicken broth

Direction

1. Chop the chicken fillet into the small pieces.
2. Then place the chicken in the air fryer basket.
3. Add diced onion and minced garlic.
4. Sprinkle the meat with the cayenne pepper and salt. Stir it.

5. Then chop the potatoes and add in the basket too.
6. Add chopped fresh cilantro and chicken broth.
7. Cook the chicken chili for 25 minutes at 360 F. Stir the chili every 5 minutes.
8. Then let the cooked chili rest for a while. Serve and enjoy!

Whole Food Meatloaf

Servings: 6

Total Time: 45 Minutes

Calories: 174

Fat: 6.4 g

Protein: 24.4 g

Carbs: 3.4 g

Fiber: 1.1 g

Ingredients and Quantity

- 1 pound ground beef
- 1 tsp. minced garlic
- 1 onion, diced
- 1 tbsp. dried dill
- 1 tsp. fresh parsley, chopped
- 1 tsp. turmeric
- 1 egg
- 1 tsp. olive oil
- 1/2 tsp. ground black pepper
- 1 tbsp. coconut flour

Direction

1. Take the big bowl and beat the egg in it.
2. Whisk the egg and add all the ingredients that were listed above except olive oil.
3. Stir the meat mixture carefully until it is homogenous.
4. Then make the shape of the meatloaf with the help of the hands.
5. Transfer the meatloaf to air fryer basket.
6. Sprinkle it with the olive oil and cook for 30 minutes at 350 F.
7. When the meatloaf is cooked, chill it a little. Serve and enjoy!

Mongolian Beef

Servings: 4

Total Time: 20 Minutes

Calories: 330

Fat: 18.1 g

Protein: 33.2 g

Carbs: 7.9 g

Fiber: 3.2 g

Ingredients and Quantity

- 16 oz. flank steak
- 3 tbsp. coconut flour
- 1 tbsp. olive oil
- 1 tbsp. coconut oil
- 1 tsp. ginger, grated
- 1 tbsp. garlic, chopped
- 1/2 tsp. salt
- 1 onion, chopped
- 1 tbsp. sesame seeds

Direction

1. Chop the steak into the cubes and sprinkle with the coconut flour and grated ginger.
2. Add garlic and salt. Stir the mixture.
3. Pour the olive oil into the air fryer basket and preheat it at 400 F for 20 seconds.
4. Then place the chopped meat in the air fryer basket.
5. Add sesame seeds and coconut oil.
6. Stir well and cook for 10 minutes at 400 F. Stir the meat every 2 minutes.
7. When the meat is cooked, remove it from the air fryer basket. Serve immediately. Enjoy!

Chicken Tenders

Servings: 4

Total Time: 19 Minutes

Calories: 247

Fat: 11.9 g

Protein: 33 g

Carbs: 0.4 g

Fiber: 0.1 g

Ingredients and Quantity

- 1/2 cup fresh basil
- 1/4 cup fresh cilantro
- 1 tbsp. olive oil
- 1 tsp. minced garlic
- 1 pound chicken fillet

Direction

1. Blend the fresh basil and cilantro in the blender.
2. Add olive oil and minced garlic. Stir the mixture.
3. Cut the chicken fillet into the medium tenders.
4. Add the basil mixture and stir it well.
5. Put the chicken tenders in the air fryer and cook them at 360 F for 9 minutes. Stir the chicken time to time.
6. When the chicken is cooked, chill it a bit. Serve and enjoy!

Pulled Beef

Servings: 4

Total Time: 45 Minutes

Calories: 235

Fat: 8.6 g

Protein: 35.4 g

Carbs: 1.8 g

Fiber: 0.5 g

Ingredients and Quantity

- 16 oz. beef roast
- 1 cup beef stock
- 1 tsp. mustard seeds
- 1 tsp. coriander
- 1 tsp. olive oil
- 1 cup water
- 1 carrot, chopped
- 1 tsp. salt

Direction

1. Chop the beef roast and sprinkle with the mustard seeds, coriander, olive oil, and salt.
2. Stir the meat and place in the air fryer basket.
3. Add chopped carrot and water.
4. Then add the beef stock and cook the meat for 35 minutes at 365 F.
5. When the time is over, transfer the meat to the bowl and shred it with the help of the forks.
6. Add the remaining liquid from the air fryer basket and stir the meat.
7. Serve immediately. Enjoy!

Low Carb Air Fryer Side Dish Recipes

Whole Food Mushrooms with Tarragon

Servings: 4

Total Time: 17 Minutes

Calories: 50

Fat: 3.8 g

Protein: 2.9 g

Carbs: 3.1 g

Fiber: 0.9 g

Ingredients and Quantity

- 13 oz. mushrooms
- 1/4 tsp. tarragon
- 1 tbsp. olive oil
- 1/4 tsp. chili flakes
- 1/2 tsp. salt

Direction

1. Slice the mushrooms and sprinkle them with tarragon, olive oil, chili flakes, and salt.
2. Stir the mushrooms and transfer in the air fryer basket.
3. Cook the mushrooms for 7 minutes at 385 F. Stir the mushrooms time to time.
4. When the mushrooms are cooked, transfer them to the bowl and chill for 5 minutes. Serve and enjoy!

Parsley Mashed Sweet Potato

Servings: 4

Total Time: 45 Minutes

Calories: 36

Fat: 3.8 g

Protein: 0.4 g

Carbs: 1.1 g

Fiber: 0.4 g

Ingredients and Quantity

- 4 sweet potatoes
- 1/4 cup almond milk

- 1 tsp. salt
- 1 tsp. dried parsley

Direction

1. Peel the potatoes and put them in the air fryer basket.
2. Cook the sweet potatoes for 35 minutes at 360 F. When the sweet potatoes are soft, they are cooked.
3. Place the cooked sweet potatoes in the blender and blend until smooth.
4. Add the almond milk, salt, and dried parsley.
5. Blend the mixture for 1 minute more.
6. Transfer the cooked meal to the serving plates. Serve and enjoy!

Curry Chickpeas

Servings: 4

Total Time: 35 Minutes

Calories: 235

Fat: 8 g

Protein: 18 g

Carbs: 4.7 g

Fiber: 2 g

Ingredients and Quantity

- 1 can chickpeas, no salt added
- 2 tbsp. vinegar
- 2 tsp. curry powder
- 2 tbsp. olive oil
- 1/4 tsp. coriander
- 1/4 tsp. cumin
- 1/4 tsp. and 1/8 tsp. ground cinnamon
- 1/4 tsp. salt
- 1/2 tsp. Aleppo pepper
- Fresh cilantro

Direction

1. Put the chickpeas in a medium bowl and smash them gently to remove the skin.
2. Add oil and vinegar to the chickpeas and toss them.
3. Add other spices and combine them well.
4. Layer the chickpeas in fryer basket and cook at 400 degrees F for about 15 minutes.
5. Shake them halfway while cooking.
6. Pour them in a bowl and add salt, Aleppo pepper and cilantro to serve. Enjoy!

Spanakopita Bites

Servings: 4

Total Time: 55 Minutes

Calories: 230

Fat: 22 g

Protein: 14 g

Carbs: 5 g

Fiber: 2 g

Ingredients and Quantity

- 1 egg
- 16 sheets phyllo cup sheets (14 x 9 inch size)
- 1 package frozen chopped spinach
- 1 cup small curd cottage cheese
- 2 cups crumbled feta cheese
- 3 to 4 melted butter

Direction

1. Preheat your oven to 350 degrees F.
2. Lightly beat the egg.
3. Take a bowl pour egg, spinach and cheese and mix all of them together.
4. Brush baking pan with some of the butter.
5. Place 1 sheet of phyllo sheet in a pan.
6. Brush your sheet with butter.
7. Layer the first sheet with 7 additional sheets and brush each sheet with butter.
8. Spread spinach mixture on the top.
9. Cover the sheet and freeze it for 30 minutes.
10. Use a sharp knife and cut into square pieces.
11. Bake for 35-45 minutes until it becomes golden brown.
12. Refrigerate the leftovers. Enjoy!

Broccoli Tots

Servings: 3

Total Time: 40 Minutes

Calories: 120

Fat: 7 g

Protein: 8.7 g

Carbs: 3 g

Fiber: 1.2 g

Ingredients and Quantity

- 12 oz. broccoli florets
- 1 garlic clove
- 1 eggs
- 1/2 cup panko
- 1/4 tsp. onion powder
- 1/8 tsp. black pepper
- 1/3 cup parmesan cheese
- Salt, to taste

Direction

1. Steam broccoli for five minutes until its tender.
2. Add all the ingredients to a food processor and pulse it until it's finally mixed.
3. Preheat the fryer to 374 degrees F.
4. Shape the mixture to tots and place them in fryer basket after greasing with cooking spray.
5. Cook for about 10 minutes until golden and crisp on the outside. Serve and enjoy!

Blueberry Lemon Muffin

Servings: 5

Total Time: 15 Minutes

Calories: 133

Fat: 6.3 g

Protein: 1.8 g

Carbs: 8 g

Fiber: 2 g

Ingredients and Quantity

- 1 cup all-purpose flour
- 1/4 cup milk
- 1/2 cup sugar
- 1/2 cup blueberries
- 1 tbsp. lemon zest
- 1 tsp. baking powder
- 2 tbsp. lemon juice
- 1 tsp. vanilla extract
- 1/2 tsp. salt
- 1/4 cup melted butter

Direction

1. Take a mixing bowl and all the ingredients to it and mix them well.
2. Spray silicone muffin molds with cooking spray.
3. Fill up the batter to 3/4 0f the mold.
4. Cook them for about 14 minutes to 320 degrees F.
5. Insert a toothpick to check if it is done from inside totally if not then cook it for more 2 minutes. Serve and enjoy!

Roasted Red Potato

Servings: 3

Total Time: 28 Minutes

Calories: 127

Fat: 4.9 g

Protein: 2.4 g

Carbs: 19.8 g

Fiber: 2.3 g

Ingredients and Quantity

- 13 oz. red potato
- 1 tsp. rosemary
- 1/2 tsp. dried parsley
- 1 tbsp. olive oil
- 1/2 tsp. salt

Direction

1. Wash the red potato carefully and cut into the cubes.
2. Sprinkle the red potato cubes with the rosemary, dried parsley, and salt.
3. Add olive oil and stir the vegetables.
4. Transfer the red potato cubes in the air fryer basket and cook for 18 minutes at 390 F. Stir the potatoes every 7 minutes.
5. Serve the cooked sweet potatoes immediately. Enjoy!

Apple Hashbrown

Servings: 2

Total Time: 30 Minutes

Calories: 172

Fat: 7.3 g

Protein: 1.5 g

Carbs: 28.1 g

Fiber: 5.2 g

Ingredients and Quantity

- 1 sweet potato, chopped
- 1 apple, chopped
- 1 tsp. ground cinnamon
- 1 tbsp. olive oil

Direction

1. Place the chopped sweet potato in the air fryer basket.
2. Add olive oil and cook the vegetables for 15 minutes at 380 F. Stir the sweet potatoes time to time.
3. After this, add the chopped apple and ground cinnamon.
4. Stir the mixture well and cook it for 5 minutes more at the same temperature.
5. Stir the cooked hashbrown. Serve and enjoy!

Squash Noodles

Servings: 2

Total Time: 25 Minutes

Calories: 63

Fat: 4.1 g

Protein: 0.7 g

Carbs: 7.4 g

Fiber: 0 g

Ingredients and Quantity

- 15 oz. spaghetti squash
- 1 tbsp. olive oil
- 1/2 tsp. dried dill
- 1/2 tsp. salt

Direction

1. Peel the spaghetti squash and place it in the air fryer basket.
2. Cook the squash for 15 minutes at 390 F.
3. After this, shred the squash with the help of the fork to make the noodles.
4. Place the squash noodles in the bowl and sprinkle with the olive oil, dried dill, and salt.
5. Stir the noodles well and serve them warm. Enjoy!

Cabbage Steaks

Servings: 4

Total Time: 19 Minutes

Calories: 61

Fat: 3.7 g

Protein: 1.6 g

Carbs: 7.1 g

Fiber: 3.1 g

Ingredients and Quantity

- 1 pound cabbage
- 1 tsp. paprika
- 1/2 tsp. ground black pepper
- 1 tbsp. olive oil

Direction

1. Slice the cabbage into the steak pieces and sprinkle with the paprika and ground black pepper from both sides.
2. Then sprinkle the cabbage with the olive oil and transfer in the air fryer basket.
3. Cook the cabbage steaks for 9 minutes at 365 F.
4. Flip the cabbage to another side after 4 minutes of cooking.
5. Transfer the cooked cabbage on the platter. Serve and enjoy!

Sautéed Kale

Servings: 4

Total Time: 18 Minutes

Calories: 117

Fat: 6.5 g

Protein: 4.5 g

Carbs: 12.5 g

Fiber: 2.3 g

Ingredients and Quantity

- 15 oz. kale, chopped
- 1/2 tsp. minced garlic
- 1 tbsp. olive oil
- 1/3 cup water
- 1/4 cup almond, crushed

Direction

1. Combine together the kale and minced garlic.

2. Add olive oil and crushed almond.
3. Stir the kale and put it in the air fryer basket.
4. Cook the kale for 5 minutes at 250 F.
5. Then add the water and cook the kale for 5 minutes more at 360 F.
6. When the time is over, stir the kale and chill to the room temperature. Serve and enjoy!

Sweet Potato Toasts

Servings: 2

Total Time: 26 Minutes

Calories: 228

Fat: 21.9 g

Protein: 2 g

Carbs: 9.3 g

Fiber: 6.8 g

Ingredients and Quantity

- 2 sweet potatoes, peeled
- 1 tsp. minced garlic
- 1/4 tsp. chili flakes
- 1 avocado, pitted
- 1 tsp. olive oil

Direction

1. Slice the sweet potatoes and rub them with the minced garlic and olive oil.
2. Place the sweet potato slices in the air fryer basket and cook them for 16 minutes at 360 F.
3. Flip them into another side after 8 minutes of cooking.
4. Meanwhile, peel the avocado and mash it.
5. Add the minced garlic and stir the mashed avocado mixture well.
6. When the sweet potato slices are cooked, chill them little and spread with the mashed avocado mixture. Serve and enjoy!

Crunchy Potato Cubes

Servings: 4

Total Time: 25 Minutes

Calories: 119

Fat: 3.7 g

Protein: 2.4 g

Carbs: 20.2 g

Fiber: 2.7 g

Ingredients and Quantity

- 1 pound potato, peeled
- 1 tbsp. olive oil
- 1 tsp. dried dill
- 1 tsp. dried oregano
- 1/4 tsp. chili flakes

Direction

1. Cut the potatoes into the cubes.
2. Sprinkle the potato cubes with the dried dill, dried oregano, and chili flakes.
3. Mix the potatoes and place them in the air fryer basket.
4. Sprinkle the potato cubes with the olive oil and cook for 15 minutes at 400 F.
5. Stir the potatoes once per cooking.
6. When the potato cubes are crunchy enough, transfer them to the serving bowl. Enjoy!

Zucchini and Carrot Slices

Servings: 2

Total Time: 28 Minutes

Calories: 105

Fat: 7.3 g

Protein: 1.8 g

Carbs: 10.6 g

Fiber: 3.4 g

Ingredients and Quantity

- 1 zucchini
- 2 carrots
- 1/4 tsp. ground cinnamon
- 1 tbsp. olive oil
- 1/2 tsp. ground paprika

Direction

1. Slice the zucchini and carrots.
2. Sprinkle the veggies with thyme, ground cinnamon, ground paprika and olive oil.
3. Shake it well and transfer to the air fryer basket.
4. Cook the veggies for 16 minutes at 380 F.
5. Stir the veggies after 8 minutes of cooking.
6. When the veggies are soft, you know they are well cooked.
7. Best served hot. Enjoy!

Green Bean Salad with Pepitas and Olive Oil

Servings: 4

Total Time: 18 Minutes

Calories: 43

Fat: 3.9 g

Protein: 0.6 g

Carbs: 2.1 g

Fiber: 1 g

Ingredients and Quantity

- 4 tsp. pepitas
- 1 cup green beans
- 1 tbsp. olive oil
- 1 tsp. sesame seeds
- 1/2 cup water
- 1/2 tsp. salt

Direction

1. Place the green beans in the air fryer basket.
2. Add water and salt.
3. Cook the green beans for 10 minutes at 390 F.
4. When the time is over, let the green beans chill little and discard them from the air fryer basket.
5. Put the green beans in the bowl.
6. Add pepitas and sesame seeds.
7. Stir the salad. Serve and enjoy!

Red Potato Salad with Chives

Servings: 4

Total Time: 28 Minutes

Calories: 164

Fat: 5 g

Protein: 4.9 g

Carbs: 26.7 g

Fiber: 3.3 g

Ingredients and Quantity

- 3 red potatoes, peeled

- 1 oz. chives, chopped
- 1 tbsp. olive oil
- 1 tomato
- 1 hard-boiled egg
- 1/2 tsp. salt
- 1 tsp. ground paprika

Direction

1. Chop the red potatoes roughly and sprinkle them with the olive oil and ground paprika.
2. Place the red potatoes in the air fryer and cook for 18 minutes at 390 F. Stir the potatoes 4 times per cooking.
3. Meanwhile, peel the eggs and chop them.
4. Place the chopped eggs in the bowl.
5. Chop the tomatoes and add the eggs too.
6. After this, add salt and chives.
7. When the red potatoes are cooked, add them to the salad bowl and stir.
8. Serve the salad. Enjoy!

Smashed Sweet Potato with Curry Powder

Servings: 2

Total Time: 38 Minutes

Calories: 44

Fat: 4.4 g

Protein: 0.4 g

Carbs: 1.6 g

Fiber: 0.6 g

Ingredients and Quantity

- 2 sweet potatoes, peeled
- 1/4 cup chicken stock
- 1 tsp. olive oil
- 1 tbsp. almond milk
- 1 tsp. curry powder
- 1/2 tsp. turmeric

Direction

1. Place the sweet potatoes in the air fryer and sprinkle them with the turmeric.
2. Cook the sweet potatoes for 30 minutes at 380 F.
3. After this, mash the sweet potatoes until you get the puree.
4. Add chicken stock and curry powder.
5. Then add the almond milk and stir the mixture until it is smooth and homogenous.
6. Serve the mashed sweet potato immediately. Enjoy!

Healthy Air Fryer Recipes for Body Size Maintenance

Sausages with Butterbean and Tomato Ratatouille

Servings: 2

Total Time: 55 Minutes

Calories: 260

Fat: 10 g

Protein: 27 g

Carbs: 23 g

Fiber: 2 g

Ingredients and Quantity

- 4 sausages

For the Ratatouille:

- 1 chopped pepper
- 2 diced courgettis
- 1 diced aborigine
- 1 diced medium red onion
- 1 tbsp. olive oil
- 440 g drained and rinsed butterbeans
- 440 g chopped tomatoes
- 2 sprigs thyme
- 1 tbsp. balsamic vinegar
- 2 chopped garlic cloves
- 1 finely chopped red chili

Direction

1. For 3 minutes, heat the Air fryer to 200C.
2. Now add the courgettis, pepper, aborigine, onion and oil and roast for approximately 20 minutes — until the veg has blistered on the skin.
3. Remove and leave to cool.
4. Turn the Air fryer down to 180C.
5. Mix the veg with the rest of the ratatouille ingredients in a saucepan and bring to a simmer before seasoning.
6. Now place the sausages to the Air fryer, make sure they don't touch each other.
7. Cook for 10 to 15 minutes and shake once during the cooking time. Serve and enjoy!

Buttermilk Chicken with Sweet Potato Chips

Servings: 2

Total Time: 37 Minutes

Calories: 190

Fat: 12 g

Protein: 30 g

Carbs: 25 g

Fiber: 3 g

Ingredients and Quantity

For the Chicken:

- 200 ml buttermilk
- 1/2 tsp. cayenne pepper
- 1 tsp. minced garlic
- Two 150 g chicken breasts
- 4 tbsp. plain flour seasoned with salt and pepper
- 1 egg
- 200 g panko breadcrumbs

For the Chips:

- 2 sweet potatoes, peeled and sliced into 1 cm thick chips
- 1 tbsp. olive oil
- 1 tbsp. sweet smoked paprika

Direction

1. In a bowl, place the buttermilk, cayenne and garlic with the chicken breasts. Cover and marinate overnight in the refrigerator.
2. Heat the Air fryer for 3 minutes.
3. Rub the marinade off the chicken.
4. Then dip the breasts into a bowl of seasoned flour, then in the beaten egg and then the breadcrumbs make sure that the chicken is well coated.
5. Place the chicken in the Air fryer for 20 minutes at 190C.
6. Toss the chips in oil and paprika and place in the Air fryer.
7. Cook at 190C for 20 minutes.
8. Season the chips with salt and pepper. Serve and enjoy!

Vegetable Crisps and Cheesy Pesto Twists

Servings: 4

Total Time: 55 Minutes

Calories: 230

Fat: 6 g

Protein: 15 g

Carbs: 18 g

Fiber: 3 g

Ingredients and Quantity

For the Vegetable Crisps:

- 2 parsnips
- 2 beetroot
- 1 medium sweet potato, peeled
- 1 tbsp. olive oil
- 1/2 tsp. chili powder

For the Cheesy Pesto Twists:

- One 320 g pack of all-butter puff pastry
- 1 tbsp. flour
- 50 g cream cheese
- 4 tbsp. pesto
- 1 egg, beaten
- 50 g grated parmesan

Direction

1. Heat the air fryer to 240C.
2. Shave super-thin strips off the parsnips, beetroot and sweet potato with a peeler.
3. Toss the vegetable slices in the oil and chili powder, then season with salt and pepper.
4. Cook in the Air fryer for 15 minutes or until crisp and golden.
5. For the cheesy pesto twists, roll the pastry into a rectangle on a lightly floured surface with its short side horizontal and the long side vertical.
6. Cut in half down the middle.
7. Spread cream cheese and pesto over one half and place the other piece of pastry on top to create a sandwich.
8. Cut in half down the middle again to create 2 large rectangles.
9. Slice each rectangle into 1 cm-thick horizontal strips.
10. Twist gently each pastry strip, pulling to lengthen.
11. Brush the twists lightly with beaten egg and scatter with Parmesan.
12. Now air fry for 20 to 25 minutes until risen and golden brown. Serve and enjoy!

Salmon with Creamy Courgetti

Servings: 2

Total Time: 15 Minutes

Calories: 230

Fat: 15 g

Protein: 32 g

Carbs: 14 g

Fiber: 2 g

Ingredients and Quantity

- Two 150 g salmon fillets, skin on
- 1 tsp. olive oil

For the Courgetti:

- 2 large sized straight courgettis
- 1 ripe avocado
- 1/2 de-stoned and chopped garlic clove
- Small handful parsley, finely chopped
- Handful cherry tomatoes
- Handful black olives
- 2 tbsp. toasted pine nuts

Direction

1. Rub and season the salmon with oil, salt and pepper.
2. Place in the Air fryer at 180C for 10 minutes until the skin turns crisp.
3. Prepare the courgetti by using a spiralizer peeler and set to one side.
4. For the sauce, chop the avocado, parsley, garlic and add some seasoning and blend in a chopper until smooth.
5. Toss the courgetti in the blended sauce and top with the salmon.
6. Scatter the pine nuts over the dish. Serve and enjoy!

Full English Meal

Servings: 4

Total Time: 30 Minutes

Calories: 310

Fat: 10 g

Protein: 26 g

Carbs: 7 g

Fiber: 1 g

Ingredients and Quantity

- 8 chestnut mushrooms
- 8 halved tomatoes

- 1 garlic clove, crushed
- 4 rashers smoked back bacon
- 4 chipolates
- 200 g baby leaf spinach
- 4 eggs

Direction

1. Heat the air fryer to 200C.
2. Season mushrooms, tomatoes and garlic in a round tin and spray with oil.
3. Place the bacon and chipolatas in the cooking basket and Cook for 10 minutes.
4. Wilt the spinach and pour boiling water through it in a sieve and drain well.
5. Add the spinach to the tin and add the eggs.
6. Lower the temperature of the air fryer to 160C and cook for a few more minutes until the eggs are cooked. Serve and enjoy!

Hot Smoked Trout Frittata

Servings: 4

Total Time: 30 Minutes

Calories: 295

Fat: 4 g

Protein: 16 g

Carbs: 3 g

Fiber: 2 g

Ingredients and Quantity

- 2 tbsp. olive oil
- 1 peeled and sliced onion
- 6 eggs
- 2 tbsp. crème fraiche
- 1/2 tbsp. horseradish sauce
- 2 fillets hot smoked trouts
- 1 handful fresh dill

Direction

1. In a frying pan, heat the oil. Then season and cook the onion on medium heat until softened.
2. Heat the Air fryer to 160C.
3. Whisk the eggs in a small bowl and add the horseradish and crème fraiche.
4. Tip the onion into a dish and add the trout and the egg mix.
5. Place dish in cooking basket and cook for 20 minutes until the frittata is golden.
6. Scatter with dill on the trout and serve. Enjoy!

Welsh Rarebit Muffins

Servings: 4

Total Time: 25 Minutes

Calories: 345

Fat: 10 g

Protein: 26 g

Carbs: 5 g

Fiber: 2 g

Ingredients and Quantity

- 8 paper muffin cases
- 1 small egg
- 2 tbsp. vegetable oil
- 75 ml milk
- 100 g plain flour
- 1 tsp. baking powder
- Pinch of mustard powder
- 40 g parmesan, grated
- Dash Worcestershire sauce

Direction

1. Heat the air fryer to 200C.
2. Double up the muffin cases to form four.
3. Beat the egg in a bowl and then add oil and milk and whisk.
4. Add flour, mustard and baking powder. Mix until the mixture is smooth.
5. Add and stir in the cheese and Worcestershire sauce and spoon the batter into the muffin cases in the fryer basket.
6. Bake for 15 minutes or until the muffins are ready. Serve and enjoy!

French Toast with Yogurt and Berries

Servings: 4

Total Time: 13 Minutes

Calories: 145

Fat: 12 g

Protein: 30 g

Carbs: 10 g

Fiber: 2 g

Ingredients and Quantity

- 2 large eggs
- 1 tsp. vanilla extract
- 2 thick sourdough slices
- Bread butter for spreading
- Mixed berries
- Squeeze of honey
- Plain low fat Greek yogurt, to serve

Direction

1. Heat the Air fryer to 180C.
2. Beat the eggs and vanilla together.
3. Butter both sides of the bread.
4. Soak the bread in the egg mix until it absorbs the mixture.
5. Now place the bread in the fryer basket and cook for 8 minutes.
6. When ready, serve with mixed berries, honey and yogurt.

Squash with Cumin and Chili

Servings: 4

Total Time: 35 Minutes

Calories: 245

Fat: 8 g

Protein: 20 g

Carbs: 7 g

Fiber: 2 g

Ingredients and Quantity

- 1 medium butternut squash
- 2 tsp. cumin seeds
- 1 large pinch of chili flakes
- 1 tbsp. olive oil
- 150 ml plain Greek yogurt
- 40 g pine nuts
- 1 small bunch fresh coriander chopped

Direction

1. Remove the seeds and slice the squash.
2. Place with the spices and oiling a bowl. Season well.
3. Heat the Air fryer to 190C.
4. Place the squash in the air fryer basket and roast for 20 minutes until soft and slightly charred.

5. In a dry frying pan toast, the nuts for two to three minutes.
6. When ready, serve sprinkle coriander over the squash and serve with yogurt and the nuts. Enjoy!

Squash with Greek Yogurt and Pine Nuts

Servings: 4

Total Time: 35 Minutes

Calories: 245

Fat: 8 g

Protein: 20 g

Carbs: 7 g

Fiber: 2 g

Ingredients and Quantity

- 1 medium butternut squash
- 2 tsp. cumin seeds
- 1 large pinch of chili flakes
- 1 tbsp. olive oil
- 150 ml plain Greek yogurt
- 40 g pine nuts
- 1 small bunch fresh coriander chopped

Direction

1. Remove the seeds and slice the squash.
2. Place with the spices and oiling a bowl. Season well.
3. Heat the Air fryer to 190C.
4. Place the squash in the air fryer basket and roast for 20 minutes until soft and slightly charred.
5. In a dry frying pan toast, the nuts for two to three minutes.
6. When ready, serve sprinkle coriander over the squash and serve with yoghurt and the nuts. Enjoy!

Salmon Fishcakes Crumb

Servings: 4

Total Time: 70 Minutes

Calories: 315

Fat: 12 g

Protein: 50 g

Carbs: 6 g

Fiber: 3 g

Ingredients and Quantity

- 250 g cooked salmon
- 400 g cold mashed potato
- 1 small handful capers
- 1 small handful chopped parsley
- Zest of 1 lemon
- 50 g plain flour, for coating
- Spray oil

Direction

1. Firstly, flake the salmon and season well by combining it with the mashed potato, capers, dill and zest.
2. Shape it into small cakes and then dust with flour.
3. Place in the fridge to chill for 1 hour to firm up.
4. Heat the Air fryer to 180C.
5. Place the fishcakes in the air fryer basket.
6. Spray with oil and cook for 7 to 8 minutes or until golden. Serve and enjoy!

Figs with Honey and Mascarpone

Servings: 4

Total Time: 20 Minutes

Calories: 243

Fat: 7 g

Protein: 34 g

Carbs: 9 g

Fiber: 3 g

Ingredients and Quantity

- 8 figs
- 25 g butter
- 3 tbsp. honey
- 150 ml mascarpone
- 1 tsp. rose water
- Toasted almonds, for serving

Direction

1. Heat the air fryer to 180C.
2. Into the top of each fig, cut across and squeeze slightly to open out.
3. Put a small knob butter in each one and place in a heat-proof dish.
4. Place the dish in the fryer basket and Drizzle over the honey.
5. Cook until the fruit has softened and the juices have caramelized.

6. Stir rosewater into the mascarpone.
7. Place a dollop on each fig and scatter the almonds over the top and serve. Enjoy!

Cod with Warm Tomato and Basil Vinaigrette

Servings: 4

Total Time: 15 Minutes

Calories: 214

Fat: 9 g

Protein: 44 g

Carbs: 6 g

Fiber: 3 g

Ingredients and Quantity

- Four 150 g cod loins
- 12 halved cherry tomatoes
- 8 halved black olives
- Juice of 1 lemon
- 75 ml olive oil
- Spray oil
- 1 bunch fresh basil, torn

Direction

1. Heat the Air fryer to 180C.
2. Spray oil on the fish loins and season well.
3. Place in the air fryer basket and cook for 8-10 minutes until flaky.
4. Meanwhile, in a small saucepan place the tomatoes and olives with the oil and lemon juice. Warm but do not boil.
5. Season and add the basil.
6. Serve with some Air fryer-cooked fries and the tomato vinaigrette. Enjoy!

Lamb Chops with Cucumber Raita

Servings: 4

Total Time: 70 Minutes

Calories: 233

Fat: 14 g

Protein: 42 g

Carbs: 3 g

Fiber: 1.5 g

Ingredients and Quantity

- 4 tbsp. natural, low fat yogurt
- 1 tsp. cumin seeds
- 1 tbsp. crushed corainder seeds
- 1/2 tsp. chili powder
- 2 tsp. garam masala
- 2 tbsp. lime juice
- 1 tsp. salt
- 4 lamb chops
- Raita, for serving

Direction

1. Combine the spices in the yoghurt add lime juice and salt.
2. Coat the lamb chops in the batter and leave to marinate for at least an hour.
3. Heat the Air fryer to 200C.
4. Place the chops in the air fryer basket and cook for 10 minutes or until cooked the way you like. Serve and enjoy!

Baked Potatoes with Cottage Cheese and Asparagus

Servings: 4

Total Time: 43 Minutes

Calories: 203

Fat: 8 g

Protein: 51 g

Carbs: 14 g

Fiber: 1.2 g

Ingredients and Quantity

- 4 medium potatoes
- 1 trimmed bunch asparagus
- 75 ml low fat creme fraiche
- 75 ml cottage cheese
- 1 tbsp. wholegrain mustard

Direction

1. Heat the air fryer to 200C.
2. Wash the potatoes and dry with kitchen paper.
3. Place the potatoes in the fryer basket and cook for 25 minutes.
4. In the Meanwhile, cook the asparagus in salted boiling water for almost 3 minutes or until just tender.
5. Allow the potatoes to cool, then slice off the tops and scoop the potato flesh into a bowl.

6. Combine with the cottage cheese, crème fraiche, asparagus and mustard.
7. Season and refill the potato skins before serving. Enjoy!

Ricotta and Spinach Filo Parcels

Servings: 4

Total Time: 50 Minutes

Calories: 222

Fat: 8 g

Protein: 20 g

Carbs: 6 g

Fiber: 2 g

Ingredients and Quantity

- 750 g large waxy potatoes
- 2 tbsp. olive oil
- 2 tsp. smoked paprika
- 150 ml low fat Greek yogurt
- 2 tbsp. Sriracha hot chili sauce

Direction

1. First of all, peel the potatoes and cut into thin wedges.
2. Soak in water for 30 minutes and then drain and pat dry with kitchen paper.
3. Heat the Air fryer to 180C.
4. Mix the paprika and oil and coat the wedges before placing into the fryer basket.
5. Air Fry for 20 minutes, shake the basket occasionally to turn the wedges.
6. Sprinkle with salt and serve with a dip made of yoghurt and hot chili sauce. Serve and enjoy!

Roasted Sprouts with Pine Nuts and Raisins

Servings: 4

Total Time: 30 Minutes

Calories: 250

Fat: 8 g

Protein: 30 g

Carbs: 10 g

Fiber: 2 g

Ingredients and Quantity

- 500 g baby leaf spinach

- 250 g ricotta cheese
- 30 g pine nuts, grated
- 1 lemon zest
- 1 egg, beaten
- 4 sheets of filo pastry

Direction

1. Boil the spinach in the boiling water for 30 seconds.
2. Drain well and squeeze out all the moisture.
3. Chop and mix with the ricotta, lemon zest, and nuts and egg. Mix well.
4. Cut each filo sheet into three strips.
5. Place 1 tablespoon mixture on the top corner of each.
6. Fold diagonally to form triangular shaped parcels.
7. Heat the air fryer to 200C.
8. Brush the parcels with some oil and place them in the air fryer basket.
9. Cook in batches for 4 minutes or until golden. Serve and enjoy!

Roast Potatoes with Bacon and Garlic

Servings: 4

Total Time: 40 Minutes

Calories: 270

Fat: 5 g

Protein: 18 g

Carbs: 4 g

Fiber: 2 g

Ingredients and Quantity

- 4 potatoes, peeled and cut into pieces
- 6 to 8 garlic cloves
- 4 to 6 striped bacon
- 2 sprigs rosemary
- 1 tbsp. olive oil

Direction

1. Take a medium size bowl for mixing, add potatoes, rosemary, garlic and bacon in it.
2. Add olive oil to the ingredients. Mix them well to get covered with oil equally.
3. Heat the Air Fryer to 200C.
4. Place everything in the fryer and cook it for 25-30 minutes, until golden brown.
5. Now put it in bowl, sprinkle rosemary and serve. Enjoy!

Roast Carrots with Cumin

Servings: 3

Total Time: 35 Minutes

Calories: 140

Fat: 3 g

Protein: 20 g

Carbs: 3 g

Fiber: 2 g

Ingredients and Quantity

- 10 medium carrots, peeled
- 2 tbsp. olive oil
- Salt and freshly ground pepper, to taste
- 1 tsp. cumin seeds
- 1 tsp. coriander seeds, chopped, for garnishing
- 1 handful fresh mint, chopped, for garnishing

Direction

1. Cut the carrots in half lengthwise. But if you find carrot fat in size, then cut it in half again for equal size of pieces.
2. Take large bowl, place carrots in it with olive oil, cumin seeds, salt and pepper. Mix all the ingredients well.
3. Heat the air fryer to 200C.
4. Cook the carrots for 20 minutes, until it become brown and tender.
5. Now dish out in a plate. Sprinkle fresh chopped mint and coriander seeds. Enjoy!

Stilton and Walnut Rounds

Servings: 3

Total Time: 70 Minutes

Calories: 290

Fat: 5 g

Protein: 30 g

Carbs: 5 g

Fiber: 3 g

Ingredients and Quantity

- 50 g butter
- 50 g plain flour

- 50 g stilton, blue cheese
- 25 g walnuts, chopped
- 1 pinch salt

Direction

1. In a food processor, add flour and salt. Mix it well.
2. Then add butter and blue cheese and again mix it until it becomes a smooth mixture.
3. Put the mixture into a bowl and put walnuts in it.
4. Now make a long roll approximate of 2 to 3cm in diameter.
5. Put a plastic film around it and freeze it for 30 mints.
6. Make a lining of parchment paper around air fryer basket and heat it up to 180C.
7. Cut the dough in circles which should be 1cm thick.
8. Now put the circles in the air fryer and cook it for about 15 minutes until it turns into golden texture. Serve and enjoy!

Crispy Potato Skin Wedges

Servings: 3

Total Time: 25 Minutes

Calories: 290

Fat: 5 g

Protein: 30 g

Carbs: 5 g

Fiber: 3 g

Ingredients and Quantity

- 4 medium size potatoes, unpeeled
- 2 to 3 tbsp. olive oil
- 2 tsp. paprika
- 1 tsp. parsley flakes
- 1 tsp. chili powder
- 1 tsp. sea salt
- 1/2 tsp. ground black pepper

Direction

1. Cut Potatoes in wedges.
2. Take large bowl, place potatoes in it.
3. Add olive oil, paprika, parsley, chili, salt, and pepper. Mix it gently.
4. Preheat air fryer to 200C.
5. Place half potatoes in air fryer basket (avoid over crowd so that they can cook well).
6. Cook them for 20-25 minutes on 200C.
7. During cooking process shake them 2 to 3 times, so that they all are equally get cooked.

8. When the color is golden brown take them out and serve them with tomato ketchup. Enjoy!

Rosemary Russet Potato Chips

Servings: 3

Total Time: 40 Minutes

Calories: 260

Fat: 4 g

Protein: 10 g

Carbs: 23 g

Fiber: 4 g

Ingredients and Quantity

- 2 medium Russet Potatoes
- 1/4 cup olive oil
- 1/2 cup sour cream
- 2 tsp. chopped rosemary
- 1 tbsp. roasted garlic
- 1 pinch salt

Direction

1. Scrub potatoes under running water.
2. Peel the potatoes and cut potatoes lengthwise on cutting board.
3. Now in a bowl full of water, soak potatoes for 30 minutes; change the water several times.
4. Preheat the Air fryer to 200C.
5. In a mixing bowl toss potato strips with olive oil.
6. Place chips into fry basket.
7. Set the timer for 20 to 25 minutes or cook until golden brown.
8. During chips are cooking pour sour cream, roasted garlic, ½ tablespoon chopped rosemary, and salt.
9. Dish out potatoes in a plate, sprinkle pinch of chopped rosemary. Serve and enjoy!

Cod Fish Nuggets

Servings: 3

Total Time: 35 Minutes

Calories: 160

Fat: 8 g

Protein: 40 g

Carbs: 5 g

Fiber: 2 g

Ingredients and Quantity

- 500 g cod fish fillet
- 1 cup breadcrumbs
- 1 cup flour
- 1 tsp. salt
- 3 beaten eggs
- 1/4 cup olive oil

Direction

1. Heat the air fryer to 200 C.
2. Take eggs, breadcrumbs and flour in separate bowls.
3. Mix the breadcrumbs with olive oil and salt.
4. Cut the fish cod approximately 1 inch strips and each strip should be ½ inch thick.
5. Now place the nuggets into flour then in eggs and finally mix it well with breadcrumbs so that they stick to nuggets well.
6. Cook the nuggets for 8 to 10 minutes. Serve and enjoy!

Peanut Butter Marshmallow Fluff Turnovers

Servings: 3

Total Time: 20 Minutes

Calories: 267

Fat: 18 g

Protein: 12 g

Carbs: 10 g

Fiber: 2 g

Ingredients and Quantity

- 4 sheets filo pastry, defrosted
- 4 tbsp. chunky peanut butter
- 4 tsp. marshmallow fluff
- 60g butter, melted
- 1 pinch salt

Direction

1. Preheat the Air fryer to 200°C.
2. Brush 1 sheet of filo with butter. Place a second sheet of filo on top of the first and also brush with butter. Repeat until you have used all 4 sheets.
3. Cut the filo layers into 4 3-inch x 12-inch strips.
4. Place 1 tablespoon of peanut butter and 1 teaspoon of marshmallow fluff on the underside of a strip of filo.

5. Fold the tip of the sheet over the filling to form a triangle and fold repeatedly in a zigzag manner until the filling is fully wrapped.
6. Use a touch of butter to seal the ends of the turnover.
7. Place the turnovers into the cooking basket and cook for 3-5 minutes, until golden brown and puffy.
8. Serve with a touch of salt for a sweet and salty combination. Enjoy!

Perfect Steak

Servings: 2

Total Time: 30 Minutes

Calories: 267

Fat: 25 g

Protein: 5 g

Carbs: 6 g

Fiber: 2 g

Ingredients and Quantity

- Two 200 g beef steak, cut
- Salt and pepper, for seasoning
- Vinegar
- Cheese/butter

Direction

1. Sprinkle salt and pepper with seasoning and add vinegar.
2. Place into a pre-heated Air fryer on 200 Degree for 15 minutes for a medium steak or 20 minutes for a well-done steak.
3. Add butter or cheese after 4 to 5 minutes.
4. Flip the steak 5 times during cooking.
5. Watching the steak in the fryer is essential.
6. Different cuts and different qualities of meat react differently to heat. Therefore the cooking time has to be adjusted accordingly. Enjoy!

Roast Chicken and Potatoes

Servings: 3

Total Time: 65 Minutes

Calories: 307

Fat: 8 g

Protein: 25 g

Carbs: 15 g

Fiber: 2 g

Ingredients and Quantity

- 1 to 1.5 kg fresh chicken
- 500 g potatoes
- 1 tbsp. olive oil
- Salt and pepper, to taste (you can marinate chicken if you wish)

Direction

1. Put chicken into a pre-heated Air fryer on 200C for 33-40 minutes depending on size of the chicken.
2. Now also place potatoes in air fryer basket and drizzle oil.
3. Potatoes need to be added to cook for at least 20 minutes.
4. Serve both together. Enjoy!

Lemon Garlic Crusted Salmon

Servings: 2

Total Time: 30 Minutes

Calories: 108

Fat: 10 g

Protein: 13 g

Carbs: 3 g

Fiber: 2 g

Ingredients and Quantity

- 6 salmon fillets
- 3 oz. butter
- 1 garlic clove, minced
- 1 large lemon
- 1 tsp. salt
- 1 tbsp. parsley, chopped
- 1 tsp. dill chopped

Direction

1. Prepare the butter mixture by heating butter over stove to liquefy.
2. Add in all spices and lemon juice and mix well.
3. Spray bottom of air fryer basket with cooking oil.
4. Place the salmon fillets in the air fryer basket, and coat salmon evenly with the butter mixture, with a brush.
5. For 15 minutes, bake in air fryer at 350 degrees.
6. Turn the fillet over midway and brush with more butter mixture for even cooking.
7. Remove from the air fryer basket when the salmon fillets are golden crusted.

8. Serve with chipotle ranch topping. Enjoy!

Spinach Cheese Stuffed Shells

Servings: 2

Total Time: 40 Minutes

Calories: 102

Fat: 15 g

Protein: 8 g

Carbs: 5.9 g

Fiber: 2.1 g

Ingredients and Quantity

- 6 oxen Jumbo pasta shells
- 1 cup ricotta cheese
- 1 cup shredded mozzarella cheese
- 1 cup chopped spinach
- 1/2 cup fresh grated parmesan cheese
- 1 egg
- 26 oz. jar pasta sauce

Direction

1. Follow the directions on the package and cook shells in boiling water and then drain.
2. Mix all cheeses, egg and spinach in a separate bowl, then stuff each shell with the mixture.
3. Spread 1/2 cup spaghetti sauce in a 7-inch deep pan.
4. Place the stuffed shells in a pan and keep the open side up.
5. Spread the remaining sauce on the top of the shells.
6. Place the pan inside the air fryer basket and bake on 275 degrees for almost 25 minutes.
7. Very carefully, remove the pan from the air fryer basket and serve with fresh garlic bread baked in the air fryer. Serve and enjoy!

Mexican-Style Air Fried Corn

Servings: 4

Total Time: 25 Minutes

Calories: 180

Fat: 3.4 g

Protein: 9 g

Carbs: 6 g

Fiber: 3 g

Ingredients and Quantity

- 4 pieces fresh corn
- 1/4 tsp. chili powder
- 1/4 cup chopped fresh coriander
- 1/4 cup feta cheese or Cotija cheese
- 1 medium size lime
- 1/2 tsp. Stone House seasoning

Direction

1. First clean the cob of your corns properly.
2. Clean the air fry basket properly.
3. Place the pieces of corn on your Air Fry Basket and cook it for 10 minutes on 390 F.
4. After completing your 10 minutes of cooking sprinkle some cheese on your corns and then again cook it for 5 minutes on same temperature.
5. Then remove it from Air Fryer Basket and sprinkle them with chili powder, Stone House Seasoning and coriander.
6. Serve it with lime wedges. Enjoy!

Whole Wheat Pita Pizzas

Servings: 2

Total Time: 15 Minutes

Calories: 230

Fat: 14 g

Protein: 11 g

Carbs: 7 g

Fiber: 3 g

Ingredients and Quantity

- 2 whole wheat pita bread
- 1/2 cup shredded whole milk mozzarella cheese
- 6 pieces large pepperoni
- 4 tbsp. marinara sauce
- 1 tbsp. chopped basil

Direction

1. First pre heat your oven on 450 degree.
2. Take your pita breads and spread marina sauce on each bread equally.
3. Now sprinkle some cheese on both of the bread.
4. Cut pepperonis into quarter and spread them evenly on pita breads.
5. Again, sprinkle some more cheese if you are a cheese lover otherwise do not sprinkle more cheese. Cook pizza for 10 minutes until crust changes its color and become golden brown in color.

7. Now serve it with topping of basil leaves. Enjoy!

Fish and Chips

Servings: 4

Total Time: 45 Minutes

Calories: 265

Fat: 6 g

Protein: 28 g

Carbs: 7.6 g

Fiber: 2 g

Ingredients and Quantity

- 1 lb. fish fillet
- 1 whole egg
- 1 cup bread crumbs
- 1 tsp. salt
- 2 potatoes
- 1 tbsp. oil

Direction

1. Cut the potato wedges and toss them with oil and salt.
2. Put the potatoes in fryer's basket and cook at 400 degrees F for 20 minutes. When done remove from basket.
3. Take a bowl and add flour, beat eggs in another bowl and pour bread crumbs in the third one.
4. Now, take the fish fillet, coat flour at first then dip in egg and at last in breadcrumbs.
5. Place fish to fryer basket and cook for 15 minutes on 330 degrees F. Flip them halfway if needed.
6. Serve with the sauce of choice. Enjoy!

Hash Brown

Servings: 4

Total Time: 31 Minutes

Calories: 103

Fat: 6.3 g

Protein: 18 g

Carbs: 5.8 g

Fiber: 2 g

Ingredients and Quantity

- 4 large potatoes, peeled and grated
- 3 tsp. garlic powder
- 1/2 cup onion, diced
- 1 egg
- Salt and pepper, to taste
- Cooking spray

Direction

1. Mix grated potato, chopped onion, and garlic, egg, salt and pepper together in a bowl.
2. Spray the fryer basket with cooking spray.
3. Place the mix to the fryer basket.
4. Cook it for 4 minutes on 400 degrees F.
5. Shake the fryer basket and cook for another 5 minutes.
6. When done, dish out and serve. Enjoy!

Whole Cornish Hen

Servings: 4

Total Time: 60 Minutes

Calories: 230

Fat: 5.2 g

Protein: 8 g

Carbs: 8.3 g

Fiber: 3 g

Ingredients and Quantity

- 1 full cornish hen
- Salt, to taste
- Pepper, to taste
- 4 to 6 green chilies paste
- 2 tbsp. olive oil

Direction

1. Take a full cornish hen and apply knife cutting on each side.
2. Take a bowl and add green chilies paste, salt and pepper and mix well.
3. Apply the mixture of spices on the Cornish hen and left it for at least 15 minutes.
4. Preheat air fryer at 390F for 4 minutes.
5. Put the hen into fryer and apply olive oil, cook each side for 15 minutes. Serve and enjoy!

Conclusion

Thanks once again for purchasing and using this *Essential Weight Loss Air Fryer Cookbook*. Achieving your weight loss target is guaranteed with the help of the recipes and health guides in this cookbook.

If you really found this cookbook helpful, please share your testimony in the amazon page of this cookbook. **Enjoy!**

CPSIA information can be obtained
at www.ICGtesting.com
Printed in the USA
LVHW060757090521
686903LV00021B/230